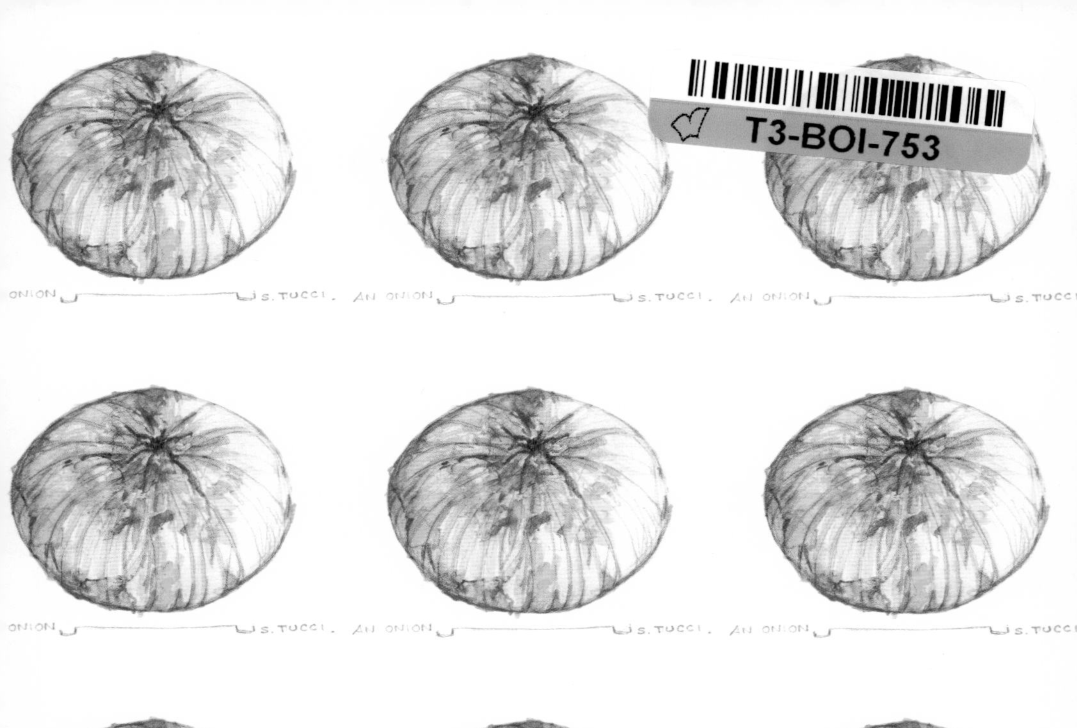
T3-BOI-753
ONION
S. TUCCI.
AN ONION
S. TUCCI.
AN ONION
S. TUCCI
ONION
S. TUCCI.
AN ONION
S. TUCCI.
AN ONION
S. TUCCI

ONION
S. TUCCI.
AN ONION
S. TUCCI.
AN ONION
S. TUCCI

ONION
S. TUCCI.
AN ONION
S. TUCCI.
AN ONION
S. TUCCI

ONION
S. TUCCI.
AN ONION
S. TUCCI.
AN ONION
S. TUCCI

What I Ate in One Year

(and related thoughts)

Also by Stanley Tucci

Taste

The Tucci Table

The Tucci Cookbook

What I Ate in One Year

(and related thoughts)

STANLEY TUCCI

GALLERY BOOKS

New York London Toronto Sydney New Delhi

Gallery Books
An Imprint of Simon & Schuster, LLC
1230 Avenue of the Americas
New York, NY 10020

First Gallery Books hardcover edition October 2024

Simon & Schuster: Celebrating 100 Years of Publishing in 2024

Interior design by Jaime Putorti

Manufactured in the United States of America

10 9 8 7 6 5 4 3 2 1

Library of Congress Cataloging-in-Publication Data is available.

ISBN 978-1-6680-5568-7
ISBN 978-1-6680-5570-0 (ebook)

To my wife, Felicity.
To my family.
To my friends.
To those I loved who are no longer at my table.

A Preamble

I never dream about food. At least there are no dreams I've had about food that I can remember. I dream about so many things, and like most people's, my dreams are wildly complex, nonsensical, and filled with twisted takes on past experiences or fears I've had or still have, like the inability to contact my wife, Felicity, or physically protect myself or a loved one.

Often, I dream that I am about to graduate high school but have avoided going to math class all year and keep hoping that I will get away with it and still be allowed to graduate. The dream is so real that I awaken in a state of terrible anxiety, believing that I will be found out, won't be able to graduate, and will need to repeat my senior year, until I suddenly realize that it was just a dream and in fact I am no longer in high school but in my sixties, and even though I am still dreadful at math, I did indeed graduate and have gone on to lead a very full life.

I also consistently have the classic "actor's nightmare." This subconscious manifestation of a deep-rooted fear entails being onstage, naked, half undressed, or in the wrong costume, filling in last minute for another actor, completely under-rehearsed, and not knowing one's lines. (Ask any actor and they will tell you they have had basically the same dream.) The irony is that I actually experienced it twenty years ago, when I was doing a play that required me to be naked for the first ten minutes or so and at least once during those ten minutes I completely forgot my lines. Unfortunately some dreams do come true.

And then, of course, there's death. I dream a lot about death. The dead. Relatives, friends, and frequently my late wife, Kate. It has been said that if we have "unfinished business" with someone or something in our lives, that event or person will visit us again and again in our dreams. I suppose it makes perfect sense. It's a way for our minds and hearts to deal with issues we've never fully dealt with.

But as I said, even though food plays a huge part in my waking life, it never plays any part in my dreams. Maybe because I don't fear it. It just makes me happy. It doesn't provoke anxiety, and in fact it may be the only significant aspect of my life that brings me peace. All others—work, children, marriage, friendships, family—bring me real joy, but I can't pretend they are not anxiety inducing. However, food is just there. A beautiful, varied thing waiting to bring satiety and solace and offer hope while death and arithmetic haunt me.

Speaking of numbers, food, and death, I've always imagined that there are three possible experiences waiting for us when we die.

> The first is that we die, and then we simply are no more. There is nothing. And that is that.
>
> The second is that we die and find that death is a long meal alone with terrible food.
>
> The third is that we die and find that death is a table resplendently set with an extraordinary meal for us and all those we've ever loved to share for the rest of eternity.
>
> If possible, when my time comes, I'll let you know which one awaits.

Tell me what you eat, and I will tell you who you are.

JEAN ANTHELME BRILLAT-SAVARIN

What I Ate in One Year

(and related thoughts)

January 2, 2023

I was sad to leave home, as it had been such a lovely holiday with Felicity and the kids, friends, and extended family. I'm headed to Rome to film *Conclave*, a movie with Ralph Fiennes, John Lithgow, and Isabella Rossellini, directed by Edward Berger. The film is based on the book of the same title by one of my favorite novelists, Robert Harris, about the choosing of a new pope. I read it a few years ago and was thrilled when I was sent the screenplay and asked to be a part of it. Excited to work with all of them. Have worked with Ralph and Isabella, and I know John a bit. Edward just did *All Quiet on the Western Front*, which was extraordinary. I had met him twice prior to filming and what a lovely fellow he is.

Relatively easy flight to Rome. Arrived at hotel/short-term-stay apartment, which I had only seen online. Some of the other cast is staying here as well. It's a "high-concept" place that is conveniently located, about a twenty-five-minute drive to Cinecittà, where we will be doing most of our filming.

My apartment is spartan at best. It is not designed with comfort in mind. It's designed with the architect's ego in mind, with which he is clearly incredibly comfortable. It consists of a living/kitchen area with a very small uncomfortable couch, a marble dining table, and a stainless-steel kitchenette against one wall. It has one rather small bedroom with a bed that looks like a bed should *look* but feels like a bed shouldn't *feel*. At least I have the small kitchen. I actually have two kitchens because I requested a connecting room for when family and friends visit, and it has a small kitchen as well. Things are looking up. Ish.

Production kindly stocked the place with staples that I requested. Pasta, both fresh and canned tomatoes, olive oil, bread, salt, butter, carrots, celery, canned beans, canned tuna, orange juice, Nespresso pods, bottled water, Tupperware, a set of chopping boards, and new knives. I asked for the Tupperware so I can transport my own food to set, as on-set catering, even in Italy, is usually questionable. More to follow on that subject.

I try not to think about spending the next eight weeks in this place. I am already missing my family and my house. Especially the kitchen. And my bed because my bed at home feels like an actual bed as opposed to those marble slabs used for making fudge.

I poured myself a glass of wine and then it suddenly occurred to me that I was hungry. The lovely people at the front desk recommended a place to eat around the corner.

I went there.

I ate.

I would *not* recommend it.

January 3

Today I unpacked properly because, as I said, I will be here for the better part of eight weeks. However, I will be flying back and forth to London whenever I have a few days free. I try to never be away from home for more than two weeks at time. The travel is tiring but it's better for my sanity and the family as a whole in the long run.

I begin rehearsals and final costume fittings on Monday, but today I just settled in, used the gym, worked on my script, and made a light lunch. Cannellini beans, canned tuna, red onion, tomatoes, and olive oil. I made a pot of tomato sauce because I find the act and aroma comforting and I know I will eat it with pasta or rice over the next few days.

I tried to get the television to work. I couldn't. I'm not very good with technology, and if this TV is as complex as the wall-mounted touchscreen panel for the lighting, which seems to have been designed by an angry astronaut, then I am going to need assistance. A lovely woman designated to help the cast with travel, errands, and technical issues such as this came up to show me how to work the television. She told me that there are no international television channels, only a few Italian ones, which I thought was weird, but lots of streamers, like Netflix, etc. Over the coming weeks I know I will indulge in my guilty pleasure, watching a spate of World War II documentaries. I can't get enough of them. I think I have seen *The World at War* a dozen times.

The weather in Rome this time of year rivals London. Actually, it's worse. Very cold and very wet.

Tonight I had dinner with my friend Claudia and her husband, Andrea. I met Claudia many years ago here in Rome and we have remained friends. I wrote about her in *Taste*, and she is featured in the Rome episode of *Searching for Italy*. We went to Taverna Trilussa in Trastevere, an ancient and now very hip part of Rome, which is much more gentrified than when Claudia first took me there thirty years ago. We sat outside under the permanent awnings and had a classic Roman meal, which means lots of pasta. We had both white and red wine and some appetizers: salami, prosciutto, and zucchini flowers stuffed with mozzarella.

I ordered the *bucatini all'Amatriciana*, Claudia the *strozzapreti Antonietta*, a thick pasta with Parmigiano, pesto, and small tomatoes. I can't remember what Andrea ordered.

There are many versions of strozzapreti, which means "priest chokers." Supposedly this pasta got its moniker because during the Middle Ages, Catholic priests felt it was appropriate to freely help themselves to the eggs harvested by their poor parishioners. This selfish act caused the parishioners, who were already lacking in just about everything, to make their pasta without eggs, resulting in a very thick pasta they would serve to the priests in the hope that they would choke to death.

Another version of this story is that the priests were just innately gluttonous and ate so much so fast that they choked to death. Which version is the truest, I don't know, but I like the fact that food, religion, and death are cojoined in the history of a single recipe.

January 4

That week I cooked at the hotel/apartment a couple of times. I stuck to my usual simple meals that consist of pasta with some sort of sauce and some greens.

I also ate in the extremely ascetic hotel restaurant. Though the place was never busy, the food always took ages to arrive, and when it did, what was put before me were small portions of some dish that was overthought, overwrought, and fussed over to the point of unrecognizability. During the course of my stay, I ended up eating there only a few times merely out of convenience and left hungry every time.

It was evident that the chef was vying for some kind of recognition from the entities that give recognition to chefs. I find this unfortunate. In film and theater, one can feel an actor trying too hard (what my teacher George Morrison used to describe as "pushing" a performance), as if to say, *Look at what depth of feeling I have!* They are *showing* us how well they are acting, instead of just simply being. They believe that this behavior will garner them awards, and unfortunately sometimes it does. But no person should ever do what they do to win awards, because their work will reek of desperation and therefore never ring true. Or, in the case of a chef, taste good.

After five days of rehearsals and fittings I flew home, as I was not to begin filming for another week.

January 16

I returned to my austere Roman accommodations on a Saturday night, during which I slept fitfully. I spent the next day exercising and memorizing lines. Unless I have someone to read the lines with me, I do this with the aid of a tape recorder. I record the other actor's lines and leave gaps for my own. And then I do it over and over and over again. Tedious but necessary. Especially as one ages. If a script is well written the lines will come easily. If not, then they don't. Actors will often blame themselves for not being able to retain certain passages or scenes, but it is often the script that is to blame because the character's thoughts don't track. By this I mean that the character isn't speaking naturally but instead the writer is using that character as a mouthpiece. In this case I always suggest a collaborative rewrite, which, depending on the egos involved, sometimes doesn't go over that well. That night I had another wonderful dinner with Claudia and her husband, who seem to know every great eatery in the Eternal City. We ate at a place called Checchino dal 1887 in the neighborhood of Testaccio. It turned out to be one of most interesting restaurants I've visited in all of Rome.

Testaccio is an area so named due to the presence of a fifteen-million-cubic-foot hill of broken amphorae built by the Romans over a period of five hundred years. ("*Testae*" means "earthenware shards" in Latin.) These amphorae held olive oil that had been transported to Rome from all over the empire. Because it was too expensive to ship them back empty to be filled again or because the residual oil was impossible to clean off, the terra-cotta vessels were broken into three sections—belly, neck, and arms—and piled carefully to create a hill. Years later it was discovered that within this man-made terra-cotta hill, when caves were dug as part of new builds, wine could be kept at a perfect temperature due to an ideal circulation system that was created by the way in which the shards were stacked. It is in one of these small caves that Checchino stores an amazing collection of wine from around the world.

The service, led by a fifth-generation family member, was effortlessly carried out, and the food was superb. I had soft, silky *carciofi alla romana* and a rich lasagna Bolognese in which years of culinary expertise were evident, an attribute that is becoming harder and harder to find in so many places these days.

January 17

I am back at Cinecittà, which translates as "Cinema City." It is a huge complex of offices and studios that was originally built by Mussolini in the thirties and has been expanded upon over the decades. At one time it housed the largest stage in Europe, stage number 5, which was Federico Fellini's preferred stage.

I first worked here about twenty-five years ago on a film version of *A Midsummer Night's Dream* in which I attempted to play Puck. I found it exciting to be working on this historic lot, but I remember being saddened by the state of the place. The grounds were unkempt, the buildings not only in need of paint but practically crumbling and their interiors unclean. I was told that the whole complex had been upgraded since then, as many more international productions were filmed there as of late, bringing in more money. I was told wrong.

Basically, it looks exactly the same. It's still in need of repairs, a fresh coat of paint, and a good scrub. A little heating might help, as it was colder inside the studio than it was outside its decaying walls.

To make matters worse, the catering is dreadful. Really. Dreadful. Gross, even. Heavy-handed sauces, overcooked pastas, stringy meats. I won't go on. I've already written about the sad state of Italian film catering in my first book, but I had hoped it might have progressed somewhat since my experience with it twenty-five years ago. All I can say is . . . alas, it has not.

Therefore, I bring my lunch every day or just make do with a banana and a small panino until the day ends and I can head to a restaurant, either alone or with one of my castmates, all of whom thankfully love food and wine. I prepare my on-set meals as follows.

Sunday, I make a large pot of minestrone and reheat it in the dressing room microwave over the course of two or three days. The second half of the week I make pasta or a risotto with marinara or sautéed vegetables and do the same. Something light but filling. I don't like to eat a lot when I am filming as it saps my energy. I save my appetite for a proper meal in the evening. Lots of water with lemon, rooibos tea, rice crackers with peanut butter and honey, and a midafternoon espresso have gotten me through many shooting days. As I'm playing a cardinal, I'm dressed in layers of heavy garments that require the help of a dresser to take on and off. This makes trips to the loo inconvenient, so the less one ingests throughout the day, the better.

January 29

I have been back and forth to Rome a few times now and besides the lousy catering, working on *Conclave* is a great experience. Edward is a brilliant director. He is patient and thoughtful. He takes the time to properly rehearse, allowing the movement of the actors to dictate the shots, and yet has a very clear vision for how he wants the film to look and can effortlessly ease an actor into doing something in order to achieve a certain shot that he has designed in advance. I'm honored to be a part of it, which is not something I say lightly.

The shooting hours are not too long, but on the days that require group scenes with many extras, they are a bit longer because it takes time to get the coverage necessary. (Basically, this means that the more people you have in any given scene, the more shots you need from various angles.) Therefore, there is a lot of waiting around.

But as a famous actor once said when an assistant director apologized for making him wait in his trailer for a long period of time (I was told it was the great Richard Harris but I can't be sure), "Please don't apologize. It's the waiting I get paid for. The acting I do for free."

I very much agree.

January 31

Isabella, John, and I went to a restaurant called L'Eau Vive that Isabella's mother, Ingrid Bergman, used to frequent. It is run by French Carmelite nuns and has been since it opened in 1969. Housed in an old palazzo, it has a small dining room on the first floor and a large one on the second (the piano nobile), where patrons sit under high vaulted, frescoed ceilings. The tables are covered with white tablecloths with much space between them. The food is classic French: onion soup, baked goat cheese with almonds, *canard à l'orange*, and so on. Each evening one or two Italian options might be offered, as well as one dish from another country—a culinary nod to the international makeup of the sisters themselves. The wine list, mostly French, is simple and, like the food, very affordable. That night the dining room was full of Romans, tourists, and a long table of priests, all eating and drinking to their hearts' content.

As we tucked in, Isabella told us that her mom frequented the restaurant because it was so off the beaten track, no paparazzi would even think to go there, and if they did, they would probably be too ashamed to try to insinuate themselves into the sisters' sacred space. In a Catholic country I suppose it's only logical that nuns would make the best bouncers.

In the middle of our entrée course, the sisters passed around a piece of paper printed with lyrics to a few hymns, all of which were in French. They then gathered at one end of the dining room and began to sing, and we were encouraged to join in. It was unexpected, it was moving, and it was beautiful.

Being part of a group of strangers from all over the globe, brought together by food, our voices raised in song beneath the fading splendor of sixteenth-century frescoes on a cold Roman night, had a profound emotional effect on all three of us. Although I was raised a Catholic, I never fully acquired the assurance of belief and therefore never really believed. Though I don't miss going to church every Sunday, I do miss the certainty of ceremony and the security of reverence. But now, in the early winter of my years, it's through nature, art, and my children that I experience reverence, and in moments around the table that I experience ceremony. All guilt-free.

I didn't want the singing to end, but like all good things, it did because it had to. There is solace in the knowledge that I can go back when I am next in Rome.

February 3

I've chosen to stay in Rome as Felicity is away, the kids are staying with my in-laws, and I'm tired after a long week of filming. My British agent and friend Oriana organized to visit me this weekend, which I've been looking forward to. She arrived tonight just as I was finishing work and we went to eat at Checco Er Carettiere, a favorite restaurant of mine that I had not been to for many years.

It has been run by the same family since Francesco (Checco) Porcelli, a *carettiere* (wine carrier), opened it in 1935. It is now run by his grandchildren and is still frequented by the glitterati, literati, *turisti*, and regular *romani*.

On certain nights there is a guitar player serenading the clientele with Italian folk songs and a smattering of foreign ditties as well. Nearly every time I've visited, this musician has been a middle-aged woman in a black dress, a white silk scarf draped around her neck, elegantly winding her way through the dining room, stopping at different tables to sing golden oldies in the language spoken by those seated there. If the table was French, she might sing something made famous by Piaf. If the table was Italian, a rendition of "O sole mio" or "Arrivederci Roma." But if the table was American, without a doubt she would sing "Country Roads" by John Denver. Why that particular song, I wish I knew. All I know is hearing those quintessentially American lyrics sung with great fervor in a thick Roman accent remains today one of the most bizarre things I've ever experienced, and will never forget. (If my publishers allow, I will sing it for the audiobook version.)

Unfortunately, tonight, there was no silk-scarved troubadour, but there was, as usual, excellent service and classically delicious Roman fare. Go there.

February 4

This morning Ori and I went to a farmers' market called Mercato di Campagna Amica al Circo Massimo, right around the corner from the hotel. It's a mouthful of a name that basically means "Country Friendly Market of the Circus Maximus." "Country Friendly" because everything that is sold comes from within a one-hundred-kilometer radius, and "Circus Maximus" because it's right across the street from the Circus Maximus. One of the largest markets in Rome, selling cheeses, meats (both cured and raw), vegetables, bread, seafood, fruit, spices, wine, and more, it's housed in a high-ceilinged room that opens to a courtyard, where fried fish and sandwiches are sold from catering trucks near a kiosk offering beer and wine by the plastic cup.

We bought a focaccia, a slice of pizza with *guanciale* (cured pig cheek, and what one is supposed to use in carbonara instead of pancetta), sheep's-milk ricotta, and honey, and sat in the courtyard sunshine that kindly peeked through the clouds for a short while. We ate the pizza, slathered the ricotta on the focaccia, and drizzled it with honey as Ori sipped a white wine and I a beer.

We cleaned ourselves up after that messy repast and wandered a bit aimlessly through the city where shards of ancient Rome punctuate the streets as magnificent but blunt reminders of civilization's fragility.

After a while we found ourselves by that astounding feat of artistry and engineering known as the Pantheon. No matter how many times I visit it, I am left breathless. Why? I remember reading a book in which that question was answered so well by the author. She wrote that when she brought her young son to visit the Pantheon, he started to cry. When she asked him why, he said, "Because it's so perfect."

There is a restaurant about thirty yards away from that hallowed dome, run by two brothers, called Armando al Pantheon, where I filmed a segment for the first season of *Searching for Italy*. Even though we had just eaten not long before, Oriana and I were hungry again, so we went there. That happens a lot when one is in Italy.

I love this restaurant because both its aesthetic and its menu sit between the elegant and the everyday, which is something we should all strive for. Without hesitating I ordered one of my favorite soups, *stracciatella. Stracciatella* is in essence an Italian egg-drop soup made with chicken broth, escarole, and, obviously, eggs.

I am a soup lover. To me soup may be the greatest culinary invention. It can be made with two ingredients or two hundred twenty-two ingredients. It can be served hot or cold. It can be cooked fast or slow. It can be eaten for breakfast, lunch, or dinner. It can be vegetarian, vegan, paleo, pescatarian, or carnivorian. It can be simple or complex. It comforts, it soothes, it refreshes, and it restores. Soup is life in a pot.

One of my favorite children's stories, "Stone Soup," is about soup. There are many versions, but this approximates the one I remember:

> A hungry soldier comes upon a town that is filled with unwelcoming, miserly residents. He knocks at a door and asks the old woman who lives there for something to eat. She says she is poor and has nothing to give him and that everyone in town will tell him the same thing and he should just move on. Despondent but not deterred, the soldier finds a kettle, builds a fire in the town square, fills the kettle with water, sets it over the fire, and places a large stone inside it. The old woman looks out

of her window and asks what he is doing, and he tells her that he is making stone soup. Curious, she comes to see for herself and is soon followed by the other villagers. They all tell him that it's impossible to make soup from a stone, but the soldier tells them that he has done it many times and that in fact stone soup is delicious. (In some versions he tells them that the stone is a magic stone.) All the villagers stand around the pot waiting to see if he is telling the truth. After a while the soldier tastes it and says it's nearly there but it could use a couple of onions to improve it. The old woman gets a couple of onions and tosses them into the pot. The soldier tastes it again and says it could use some garlic, and a villager runs to get garlic. This continues with carrots, parsnips, celery, beans, a chicken, herbs, and so on until the kettle is filled with a hearty soup that the soldier shares with the villagers. Soon they realize that it wasn't the stone that made the soup so delicious, but the ingredients they all shared to make it. After this, they are no longer miserable and parsimonious, but happy and generous.

I think it's one of the best stories about how man treats his fellow man (badly in the case of the villagers and kindly in the case of the soldier). But it's also about how food not only brings people together but makes life better.

Anyway, I ordered the *stracciatella* and it was everything I wanted it to be. For my main, I ordered the carbonara (I guess I felt I needed more eggs), and it was scrumptious. Oriana ordered the *Amatriciana*, which was equally as good. When we finished gorging, we shared a look that silently asked each other, *Why and how did all that go into our bodies, and do you think they have a place in the back where one could just lie down for an hour or so?*

After an espresso, we took a long stroll to minimize the damage done by our lack of restraint at the table. We wandered past the Vittorio Emanuele II monument, an ill-proportioned white marble monstrosity that looms over Piazza Venezia, known by the locals as "the wedding cake" or "the typewriter" because it resembles grotesque versions of both, and made our way to the Spanish Steps, which I happen to think are beautifully proportioned. Eventually, after shuffling off our postprandial sloth, we found ourselves at the rooftop bar of the Hotel Eden with martinis in hand watching the day disappear over Rome.

February 16–19

Felicity and the kids came to visit and, at the risk of sounding too sentimental, I felt whole again. The evening they arrived, we went to a lovely restaurant that I had been to before called Sora Lella, just walking distance from the hotel. It is run by the grandson of Elena Fabrizi, who opened it in 1959. Born in 1915, she had been an actress of some note throughout her life, and her brother was the famous Italian actor Aldo Fabrizi, but she loved to cook, so she and her husband (who worked in an abattoir) started this restaurant. The menu, like the owners, is very Roman: *guanciale*-based tomato sauces and various offal, such as sweetbreads, tripe, and *pasta con pajata di vitello a latte*. The latter is one of my favorite Roman dishes and something I order repeatedly while I am there.

The sauce is made with the intestine of a baby calf that is slaughtered while the mother's milk is still inside of it. (Apologies to the fainthearted.) The intestine, its contents, and the light tomato sauce they are cooked in give the dish a singular flavor that is at once sweet and slightly sour. I first had it many years ago, but it was on this trip that I really came to appreciate not only the delicacy of it but also its brilliance. Again, the poor Romans made something extraordinary tasting as well as nutritious out of what most others might carelessly discard.

Having been to Sora Lella a few times myself, I wanted to take Felicity and the kids there, because the staff were so kind and I knew they would welcome the kids heartily, which they did. We ate a great deal that night, although Millie was a bit picky and just ate her usual handfuls of prosciutto and bread, followed by pasta with butter and cheese. Matteo was more adventurous and devoured his first arancini along with some *pasta alla marinara*. I must attempt to make arancini for him because he keeps talking about them. However, I know that his response will be something like, "They're just not quite the same as the ones in Rome." Maybe I won't make the attempt. As an actor I have suffered too much rejection over the years. Why go begging for it?

We took a tour of the Colosseum, which was wonderful but a bit long for four-and-a-half-year-old Millie, even though she had a carton or two of breadsticks to keep her occupied. After she took her first bite and showered the ancient floors with crumbs, the legion of pigeons who frequent that ruin followed Millie (now known as Gretel) and remained her devoted companions for the rest of the tour.

On the last night of their stay, I made some pasta, and we ordered in a pizza at Matteo's request as we had been out and about all day and everyone was too tired to eat out again. I asked the kids to make some drawings of what they had seen over the last couple of days. Matteo drew gladiators in the Colosseum, and Millie drew a view of the Colosseum surrounded by grass and sky that would make any artist wish they could draw with such assurance and beautiful, poetic naivete. Like my father, an art teacher, did with us when we were children, I have always encouraged my children to draw and paint. Though you all may be working separately, there is a bond that is silently happening between you. Sharing each other's drawings when you've finished is the completion of that bond.

I was so happy to have them all there. Due to my career choice, the consistency of "normal" family life is impossible. Dinner at a certain time, helping with homework, going to school activities or sports matches, bedtime stories, and so on, what we might consider the mundane. The hardest part of being an actor is finding that family/work balance. This is true in so many professions, but it's the distance apart for long periods of time and the constant changing of shooting schedules and locations that make it even more difficult. Some actors will bring their family with them on many if not all jobs. The kids will be either put into a local school or homeschooled. I think this is fine every now and again, and in fact, I have done it a number of times over the years and have found it to be a very positive experience for the kids. But fundamentally I believe that children want and need consistency of place and people. It keeps them grounded and secure. *I* chose this profession, *they* did not, and therefore it's up to me to travel back and forth as often as possible. That said, having them there for those few days, my strange soulless apartment was transformed into a home. It was my happiest time in Rome.

February 20–March 8

Working in Rome continued like this for the next few weeks. I mostly cooked at home as I was working every day, but if we didn't wrap too late and I wasn't too tired I would find a castmate to dine with or have a quick meal out alone.

Ralph, a true food lover, and I ate together several times, diving headlong into Roman dishes accompanied by bottles of red from the most northern parts of Italy, like Alto Adige or Friuli. We realized we both preferred these regions' softer, less tannic reds to the stronger reds of middle and southern Italy. Most men prefer heavier, "meatier" wines with lots of tannins. Due to insufficient saliva (a lingering effect of radiation treatments), anything that is too tannic is nearly impossible for me to drink, so I have found my way to soft, silky pinot noirs and the like and am happy with them. I was also happy to get to know Ralph. We had worked together before, on *Maid in Manhattan*, over twenty years ago, and very briefly on *The King's Man* a few years back. We had only ever socialized a few times, so filming gave us the opportunity to spend time one-on-one, which was a great pleasure as he is talented, is smart, is thoughtful, and (as I said) loves good food and drink, which might be the most important criteria for a friendship. And so now, at an age when one doesn't necessarily make many new friends, I have done so.

We ate together at many places in Rome, the wonderful, aforementioned Taverna Trilussa being one of them, but one of our last meals was at a restaurant that has a particularly fond place in my stomach and my heart: Pommidoro. I have written about Pommidoro in *Taste*, having discovered it while filming *Searching for Italy* and fallen in love with its owners and its history. This eatery in the San Lorenzo neighborhood of Rome has only just reopened at the beginning of this year due to the death of its elderly owner a few years ago. Luckily his son, who runs it, and his grandson, who has taken his place proudly behind the huge gas range, have brought this historic family restaurant back to life. A week before they were to open, they reached out through production and said they wanted to throw a pre-opening party for me and however many people I wanted to bring by way of thanking me for featuring them on the show a few years back. I made it clear that there was no need to thank me at all as I considered it a great honor as well as an education for me to have spent time there at all, but in usual Italian fashion they would not take no for an answer.

So, I accepted, and my producing partner and right hand/left brain, Lottie, and I put together a group of about fifteen of us from the series, and we were treated to some of the best food in Rome: *carciofi*, sweetbreads, lamb chops, and tastings of three classic Roman pastas: *alla gricia*, *all'Amatriciana*, and the house specialty, *spaghetti alla carbonara*.

How happy were our hosts and how happy was I to see how happy my colleagues were as they discovered bite by bite the treasures of the Pommidoro family kitchen? Well, very happy indeed.

March 1

While I was on my way home after a long day of filming, I stopped at Circoletto, a little wine bar/restaurant around the corner from my hotel. I had always wanted to go in as it looked quite different from a lot of others in the area, but I never had. It was a casual place filled with a younger crowd (well, just about any crowd is younger to me these days, unless I'm visiting a nursing home) that seemed to be comprised of mostly Italians. I ordered a glass of wine at the long counter from one of the owners, a young fellow with lots of "tats," who was extremely excited about my presence, to put it mildly. Practically jumping up and down, he told me I had to try one of his sandwiches. I told him I had just eaten (meaning I had hurriedly ingested the remains of that day's lunch before leaving set), but he insisted that I try his sandwich, and I insisted that I really was quite full, and then he insisted some more, and then his brother came over and also insisted, and the guy sitting next to me, who was a friend of theirs, also insisted, and being outnumbered and at this point exhausted, I had no choice but to acquiesce. Within moments, a warm sandwich of ox tongue, homemade pickles, and a delicate mayonnaise on toasted bread was placed before me. Because of my difficulty eating meat (again, due to a lack of saliva), I was hesitant to try it, for fear of choking, but I did. I've never made a better decision. I've also never been so glad to be bullied into eating something. It was delicate and rich and like nothing I had ever eaten in Rome. It was a wholly new thing made with classic Roman ingredients prepared in totally new ways. Then the brothers, whose names are Nicolò and Manuel, served me an artichoke, *alla giudia* (yum), and another glass of wine, then I ate something else (I can't remember what, but it was great), and then I was angry at myself for letting my entire stay go by without having walked through these doors to sit at this culinary oracle disguised as an ordinary wine bar.

March 3

I completed work on *Conclave*. I have now left my performance in the capable hands of the director and editor, something that always makes any actor a little nervous. Sometimes what one thinks will be an integral scene or moment in a film ends up on the cutting-room floor. Although since we no longer use actual film, the cutting-room floors are free of celluloid snippets. Now all those moments just disappear into the digital ether. Working with people who are great at what they do is a joy and doesn't happen as often as it should. I'm sad that it's over yet excited to be going back home for a bit. But first Felicity and I spent a few days together on a tropical isle with my sister- and brother-in-law, Emily and John, and some friends to celebrate Emily's fortieth. (I met her when she was twenty-two. Christ. Why doesn't this "time passing" thing stop for a while?) John had organized the event perfectly, and it was a good time with good weather, good food, and good friends. After two months of wearing a cardinal's cassock in a cold, damp, dreary Rome, the sun, sand, and sea were just what I needed. I didn't want to leave.

March 27

I had a lunch meeting at the Italian embassy with the ambassador to the UK, Inigo Lambertini, and Chef Francesco Mazzei. I had met the ambassador before, and I have known the talented Francesco for more than ten years. Felicity and I had one of our first dates at a restaurant of his and we eventually held our wedding reception dinner there a couple of years later.

Ambassador Lambertini had invited us to discuss throwing a lunch or dinner for the king and queen, something that is often done by ambassadors when a new monarch is crowned. When the ambassador had extended the invite to King Charles, HRH told him that he would indeed come, "but only if Stanley Tucci is invited as well."

What can I say, dear reader. Such is my lot in life.

Of course, I was extremely flattered, but I soon got over myself (almost) and set to the task of figuring out how we might orchestrate the event. Dishes, venues, seasons were discussed, and in the end, we decided to serve four courses, alternating between Italian and British recipes that complemented one another, and hoped that the king and queen would enjoy the positive bicultural sentiment as well as the food itself.

March 28

Went to Rochelle Canteen for a book launch for one of Felicity's clients, Claire Ptak. She owns Violet Cakes in London and has written a book called *Love Is a Pink Cake*. I'm not a "dessert person"—I prefer to end a meal with an espresso or a *digestivo*—but it really is a gorgeous book. Rochelle Canteen, owned by Melanie Arnold and Margot Henderson (the famous British chef Fergus Henderson's wife), is situated off the beaten path not far from Liverpool Street. Hidden behind high brick walls, the restaurant is small but opens onto a covered outdoor area. Once you enter this indoor/outdoor space, London disappears, and no matter what, the weather, place, and time become vague. What exists is only the casual elegance of the space and those inhabiting it at that moment. I felt as though I were in an impressionist painting brought to life even though none of the clothing the patrons wore, nor the décor, suggested as much. Maybe it was just the light or the lightness of touch in the design and the food. The seasonal menu is fresh and thoughtful but not fussy. Here it is:

LOVE IS A PINK CAKE BOOK LAUNCH
28/03/2023

MENU

Blood Orange, Kohlrabi & Buttermilk Dressing
Roast Winter Tomatoes, Little Gem & Anchovy Salad
Potted Shrimp, Pickles & Toast
Bread

Braised Lamb Shoulder, Shallots & New Season Garlic
Turnips & Greens

Claire's Rice Pudding & Rhubarb

Bird in Hand Sparkling 2020
Bird in Hand Chardonnay 2016
Bird in Hand Syrah 2020

BIRD
IN
HAND

Special thanks to Square Peg and Wild at Heart flowers

Rochelle Canteen

April 5

We flew to Florida to visit my parents. Having the vibrant energy of little children in their home brought such joy to both of them and to my sister Gina, who lives with them during the winter. My mother overfed all of us, which brought her even more joy. My father was stronger than when I last saw him a few months before. He joined us at the beach one day although it was not easy for him to make his way on the soft sand. For the most part we did little to nothing except eat and take Millie and Matteo to one of the small communal pools that are part of the sprawling condo complex where my folks live. We splashed about with them, played the loudest games of Marco Polo the condo residents have probably ever heard, and helped Matteo as best we could to capture and hold chameleons for hours on end. Over our five-day stay, my mother made various pasta dishes from her repertoire: chicken cutlets, lamb chops, escarole with beans, and of course pizza and focaccia, especially for Matteo and Millie. I loved watching them eat what their older siblings and I grew up eating. All those wonderful dishes that date back countless generations, born of poverty, still endure in the digital age, nourishing bodies young and old and solidifying the connections between them. The food she served during our stay was what she also served to my older kids when they would stay with her and my father. But like most grandparents, she has been much more willing to cater to each child's needs for every meal than she was when my sisters and I were young. This makes sense given the fact that she had a full-time job and then came home and cooked an amazing three-course meal every night. But that is something a grandparent doesn't do. The grandparent indulges the grandchild's desires. That's one of the reasons why kids usually love going to visit them. But nowadays we often parent our children like *we* are their grandparents. This throws off a familial balance that has been securely in place for generations. Anyway, whether we indulge them a bit or not, what's important is that they learn to love home cooking. Home-cooked food strengthens our bonds when we are together, keeps us connected when we are apart, and sustains the memory of us when we have passed away.

April 12

Back in London. Another Zoom meeting with another company to find a new home for *Searching for Italy*, or whatever we're going to rename it because for legal reasons we cannot use the same name. Luckily there is lots of interest. Had fittings for the upcoming UK junket for *Citadel*, a series for Amazon I filmed last year. Celebrated my publicist Jenn Plante's birthday at our house with Lottie. We made risotto, steak, and salad, and Jenn ate heartily. When we started working together twenty-five years ago, she had the diet of a petulant six-year-old. "I don't eat that" was her response to almost every food except the blandest. Luckily, after spending a lot of time with me, she now has a much more varied diet. But she still hates to cook. We will get there whether she likes it or not, because I will always be in her life, whether she likes *me* or not.

April 13

Did *Citadel* press. Richard Madden and his friend Cheryl Calegari came over and we ate more steak and pasta. They brought a chocolate cake that was one of the most delicious, sweet things I have ever tasted. Richard is very strict about his diet due to all the physical roles he plays, yet he still ate two helpings of pasta, steak, and half the cake. That made me happy. He was happy too. At one point during the evening, at his insistence, we experimented with "hyperdecanting" a bottle of wine by putting it in a blender for a few moments. Did it work? I think so, but the chocolate cake I'd eaten was confusing my palate. Must try again.

April 15

Flew to Scotland to meet Joe Russo at his daughter's alma mater, St. Andrews. The Russo brothers, Joe and Anthony, have started a film festival on campus for the students and community. They asked me to screen *Big Night* and give a talk afterward with Joe. Joe was as articulate as usual, and the students' questions were intelligent, thoughtful, and very much about cinema and not celebrity and all that nonsense. I was so impressed because this is not usually the case. I want to go back there and teach a class. (I have taught classes and workshops over the years as well as worked as an advisor to young filmmakers at the Sundance Lab for many summers and have found it so rewarding. I often think I learn more than the students themselves.)

I also want to go back to eat the fish and chips I had in the pub connected to the hotel I stayed in overlooking the famous St. Andrews links. It was some of the best I've ever had, and after a decade in the UK I think I can say this with great authority. I might have to take up golf, so I have an excuse to go back. Or I'll just go back. I have no desire to play golf. I'd rather be flayed.

Also had a great Italian meal with the Russo family and friends in town at a place they have gone to many times. Really, really good. Had eggplant parmigiana and it was delicious. There is a substantial Italian immigrant population in Scotland and as far as I'm concerned that is never a bad thing for any country.

April 20

In the airport lounge I ate a croissant that was rather good. I attempted to eat some overbaked Tater Tot–like things and a spoonful of the slurry that the Brits call baked beans, but I failed because they were gross.

The flight departed late. Once in the air, I realized I was hungry due to the delay, so I ate the cold prawn appetizer, which was benign but well cooked and not mealy like prawns can be when *too* well cooked. On the left of my tray sat a small bowl of golden mush with some sort of purplish-red compote sitting atop, which caused confusion for me and my row mate, a middle-aged woman who was reading *The Little Coffee Shop of Kabul.* As I examined the stuff, she muttered to me in a cockney accent, "I have no idea what that might be but it doesn't look very *appetizin'*." I agreed and suggested it might be hummus. She shrugged and so did I.

I dared a taste. It had little or no flavor, not even a hint of tahini, only the gritty dryness of ground chickpeas, but I was still unsure. I could feel my fellow traveler staring at me awaiting my opinion. I turned to her and shrugged again. She smiled and went back to her book. I cautiously tasted the compote that adorned the mush and decided it was a cooked-to-death, very sweet version of caponata. Caponata is a Sicilian sweet-and-sour ratatouille of sorts with peppers, eggplant, tomatoes, sultanas, vinegar, sugar, celery, pine nuts, and so on. Normally, when well-made, it is quite delicious. This was not well-made, nor delicious.

Diving in once more, I realized that the golden mush was indeed a chickpea mash. In fact, I was *more* than sure, because very soon afterward my stomach reacted as it usually does when I've eaten chickpeas. I ordered a scotch to settle things, regretting that I hadn't bought a protein bar or something before boarding so I wouldn't have to eat the airplane food. I decided that a good workout was in order upon arriving at the hotel to make me well again.

After checking in, I was ushered into my fifth-floor suite, which sported an outdoor terrace large enough for a small wedding. I called my daughter Isabel in her room; she was employed as my groomer, meaning my makeup artist, on the tour in both London and Rome. ("Groomer" is a terrible word. It likens the actor to a horse and the makeup artist to a sexual deviant.)

Anyway, I asked her to come and enjoy the sunshine that blessed my terrace, as neither of us has seen the stuff for months because we live in London, where the sun insists on making itself a stranger. Lottie joined us a few minutes later. My promise to hit the gym was swiftly broken soon after checking in, because the Roman sun and a complimentary bottle of Franciacorta quickly squelched my desire to exercise. I popped the cork and the three of us sipped its dry, understated effervescence as the American songbook played through my iPhone, which sat in a coffee cup amplifying the sound.

I need to get a speaker.

Dinner that night was at Piatto Romano with Richard and some of his team. It is now a famous, informal eatery in the Testaccio neighborhood, where I had been only a couple of months before while filming *Conclave*. The food is great, but for me, this time around the highlights were the appetizers.

They were as follows:

Fava beans with sautéed greens and *guanciale*: A perfect combination. The beans savory, the *guanciale* lending a strange sweetness.

Baby zucchini marinated in vinegar and sugar for three days: delicate and delicious.

Tiny *carciofi alla giudia*: These are the ubiquitous fried artichokes of Rome that were originally cooked by the Jewish population and eventually became a favorite of all Romans. As has unjustly happened again and again for centuries, Jews were segregated to the ghetto by papal decree in 1555. Because so much of Rome and its environs were not accessible to them, they were reduced to eating the off cuts and offal of animals and whatever they could cultivate or gather from their surroundings. Out of very little, they created some of the best food the city has to offer to this day.

Artichokes are abundant throughout Lazio, the region in which Rome proudly sits, and are eaten practically every day in myriad ways when in season. The two most popular recipes are *carciofi alla romana* and *carciofi alla giudia* ("*giudia*" is Italian for "Jewish"). It has been said that because the Orthodox kitchen demands the separation of dairy and meat and veg, the Jews of Rome came up with a way to fry the artichokes in olive oil instead of butter, thus creating this delicacy. I find that odd, however, as butter is not often used in Lazio, or for that matter south of Bologna or Turin. All we know is that *carciofi alla giudia* are addictively delicious when cooked properly, and these were exactly that. They were served in a paper bag, like popcorn but profoundly better.

April 22

A couple of days later we left Rome and were jetted to Los Angeles. Please don't get the idea that I am constantly on private jets. The company that is producing the show is a wealthy one and they make use of them, as they are more efficient when a schedule is tight. The catered food on the plane was unremarkable but the wine was good. We talked and ate and sipped, then slept and ate and talked and sipped again for the almost seventeen hours it took to get from one of the oldest cities in the world to one of the newest. The reason for the delay was the fact that the French air traffic controllers were on strike, and apparently we needed them to usher us over their *pays*. We were told that, like the rest of their countrymen, they were on strike because Macron had raised the retirement age from thirty-five to thirty-six or something like that.

Landing in LA deliriously tired, Lottie and I checked into our hotel, cleaned up, and walked across the street to Sugarfish. It's a small Japanese place that serves a limited menu of what they call "old-style sushi." There is no miso soup or bowls of rice, soba noodles, or salads, only sushi and nigiri. The fish was as fresh as any I've ever tasted, the rice warm and almost sweet, and the soy sauce dark and creamy. A small bottle of cold sake and about six small plates of various raw fish filled us up in no time. After a few days in Italy eating lots of pasta, it was a welcome respite.

* * *

The screenings and press events went well over the next few days. During a break Lottie and I had lunch at Il Pastaio, a restaurant owned by the Drago family, who have had and still do have a number of places in LA for close to fifty years. It was to one of their original places that I was taken by my then agents on my first trip to LA almost forty years ago. I remember it distinctly because it was an oasis in a city that I disliked right away. The scope of Los Angeles was overwhelming, especially when navigating one's way using a Thomas guide. Thomas guides are described by Wikipedia as "paperback spiral-bound atlases." *Atlases!* Not just *maps*! This guide was the only way to get to where you were going and not end up in Vancouver or Guadalupe. I had general meetings and auditions every day all over the city and was probably late to every one of them because I got lost so often. Every time I set out on the road, I did my best to avoid making a left turn because there was so much traffic coming in the other direction. This made every trip easily twice as long as it would have normally been. I barely ate for days, and if I did eat, it was typically at drive-through fast-food joints because I was afraid of being even later if I parked and went into a restaurant. I hated it. I think I lost ten pounds in two weeks. The best thing about it all was staying with my cousin Steve and his now husband, also named Steve, and getting to spend time with them.

Anyway, that first business meal I had at a Drago family restaurant was squid-ink risotto with shrimp that was delicious. Even in Italy all these years later I have found it hard to rival. I thought about ordering it this visit but opted not to as the squid ink would blacken my teeth, rendering me silent and unsmiling for the rest of the day's press. Instead, I ordered the *paglia e fieno* pasta with zucchini, basil, garlic, Parmigiano, and a bit of butter.

"*Paglia e fieno*" means "straw and hay." It is a combination of two different kinds of tagliatelle, one made with flour and egg and the other with the addition of spinach. The yellow ribbons suggest the straw and the green give the impression of dried strands of hay, hence the name. It was quite good and reminiscent of *spaghetti alla Nerano*, a dish from Campania with similar ingredients.

Lottie had pasta with broccolini and sausage, which she enjoyed, and although I never asked her for a taste, I was convinced it was not as good as my own.

April 26

New York City, last day of press tour.

After being in Los Angeles, I was thrilled to be back in the Big Apple, where I had lived for many years when I was younger. The streets were alive with pedestrians, as opposed to those in LA, which are mostly devoid of humans using their legs for their intended purpose. And unlike the arid, dusty air of Los Angeles, New York's had moisture and depth (which might sound gross, but it wasn't). As we made our way into Manhattan and I looked upward, the familiar buildings seemed to have stretched themselves even higher since the last time I passed by them. Manhattan. *The* City. New York, New York. The city so nice they named it twice.

We arrived in the evening and checked into the Crosby, a lovely hotel owned by the Firmdale hotel group (more about another one later). The Crosby is unsurprisingly located on Crosby Street in SoHo, a neighborhood now completely different than it was when I moved to Manhattan in 1982. At that time, SoHo was nothing but "lofts" once used for manufacturing, in gorgeous mid-nineteenth-century cast-iron buildings. In the early 1970s, artists began to populate them because of their massive square footage, twenty-foot-high ceilings, and dirt-cheap prices. By the early 1980s, even though the number of tenants had increased, and galleries had already begun to occupy the storefronts, I remember the neighborhood having very little in the way of shops and restaurants, and come nine p.m., the streets were relatively empty. But within a few years after my arrival, there were countless galleries, eateries, clothing stores, and so on. (This had nothing to do with my arrival.) This gentrification inevitably forced many of the artists to move as rents increased or buildings were turned into co-ops or condominiums that they could ill afford.

Although nowadays it is a lovely area where every square inch of real estate is coveted, I do miss its less-refined state. The streets were quiet after dark, and one could amble among the cast-iron and stone edifices and through the shadows of fire escapes cast by the dim lights above the cobblestone streets. I loved that those cobblestones were Belgian block brought over as ballast on merchant ships from Europe and put to brilliant use paving the streets of a place that would become one of man's most significant creations. It is partly because of that history that I couldn't wait to move to New York when I was young. It wasn't just the never-ending newness and energy of the city that I sought like so many young people, but also its past. It's one of the reasons I love London, a city whose history stretches back far beyond that of New York's, by two millennia. The Romans founded the first substantive settlement, Londinium, around 47 AD, although traces of settlements thousands of years prior have been found on the site. In fact, there is still wild rocket (arugula) that grows in nooks and crannies throughout the city because it was brought there by the Romans.

Quite simply, I am drawn to the past more than I am the future. I don't want to rocket (the engine-propelled kind) into space or live on another planet. I don't want my phone to be able to do more than it already does or for my watch to tell me my heart rate or other people's thoughts. I am analog. Not only do I want to be *in touch* with the moment as it unfolds without being made hyperaware of every aspect of it by some device but I also want to *actually touch*. I am physical, kinesthetic, tactile. Through touch, I take in information. Today what we predominately touch are the screens on our devices. This touch has practically eclipsed all others. In short, we have become less tactile, and in the future, we will become even less so. I don't want that future. I don't want that world. I don't mind getting my hands dirty. I want to dig a hole in the earth and find the remains of something that was once something of importance, no matter how minor, to someone many years ago and imagine what their life was like. It's why I love mudlarking along the Thames foreshore. Exhuming remnants of past lives holds endless fascination for me. Therefore, the older a city is, the better. Yet I have just written this anti-tech rant on a computer with spell-check and a thesaurus. I also just had to look up how to spell "thesaurus." I went to "tools," which is where *Thesaurus*, the informative dinosaur, lives.

Anyway, after freshening up at the hotel, we made our way to Raku, a popular Japanese restaurant within walking distance. I started with a delicate egg-drop soup, and we all ate chicken-and-vegetable dumplings. Seared Wagyu beef was next. I tried a piece, hoping I could eat it, but my dearth of saliva prohibited me from doing so. However, I was able to swallow about half of it and get a good dose of its rich, fatty flavor. Begrudgingly I let those who could fully enjoy it finish the rest.

April 27

I awakened, not knowing what city I was in, and exercised as usual, but I ate practically nothing as I was rushed to two interviews in different parts of Manhattan.

The first was a live show, *The View*, on which I had not appeared for years, but it was enjoyable. (How cool and smart is Whoopi Goldberg?)

The second was a longer taped interview with Willie Geist for his *Sunday Today* show. I had not met him prior to this, but coincidentally he bought my house in Westchester when I moved to London over ten years ago. Willie and his wife purchased it as a weekend home, but it has since become their full-time residence. He showed me a picture of the kitchen, which he altered a bit over the years, and I was subsumed by memories of my life in that place.

My late wife, Kate, and I bought it together and raised our children there for five years until her death in 2009. We renovated and added a new master bedroom and playroom, and turned a small barn into two proper stables for her horse and an annoying pony. We planted dozens of pine trees to shelter us from the road; cleared land for two small paddocks; planted three apple trees, one for each of our children, and some river birches; and renovated the pool and patio area.

Most important, we created a huge kitchen/dining/sitting area, which opened onto the patio, where we built an outdoor kitchen with a wood-burning pizza oven. It was the most wonderful combination of indoor and outdoor cooking spaces, in which we hosted so many parties, dinners, and holidays all the year round.

It is the house from which I watched my children leave for their very first days of school, the house where we learned of their mother's illness, the house in which she passed away, and the house that overlooks the magnolia tree where some of her ashes are scattered.

It is the house where Felicity came to live with me and my children and where we shared many meals with family and friends both old and new.

It is the house by the ancient oak underneath which Felicity and I were married, and the house where her family, my family, and Kate's father spent our first Christmas together.

It is the house that, with great sadness and nervous anticipation, my kids and I waved goodbye to as we set off to create a new life with Felicity in England.

It is the house where the Geist family now eat their meals and celebrate their holidays, and the house in which their memories now live beside ours.

After the interview with Willie Geist (whom I now loathed because he was living in my house. Kidding. Maybe), I returned to the hotel, finished packing, changed my clothes, and met Lottie in the hotel restaurant. We ordered a smattering of small plates, all of which were just . . . okay. The Cuban sandwich would have been excellent had they not slathered it with so much Dijon mustard that it was eye-wateringly difficult for anyone to eat.

Richard arrived soon afterward, and we ordered martinis to celebrate the end of a long press tour. As a lark we filmed our martini toast for Instagram, and a few days later our followers as well as the press interpreted it as a cheeky hint that Richard would soon be playing James Bond, as his name had been bandied about as Daniel Craig's successor for a while.

That night I ate nothing on the flight home except a sleeping pill, which fulfilled its mission.

April 28

I arrived home in time to see the kids before school. They departed moments afterward under the care of our nanny, who, along with Felicity, more than picked up the slack while I was away.

I scrambled some eggs, fried up some *prosciutto cotto* (cooked sliced Italian ham), slapped it all between two pieces of lightly toasted white bread from the 1950s-era bakery around the corner, wolfed it down, and then collapsed into bed for longer than I had anticipated.

Obviously, the sleeping pill decided that it had not completely fulfilled its mission.

In the evening, after the children ate *pasta con pesto*, I steamed mussels in white wine with shallots and garlic, dressed them with olive oil and parsley, and served them with toasted French bread. I also made spaghetti with fresh tomato sauce for me because I was hungrier than I'd realized. Felicity declined my offer to join me for a bit of it. I'm not sure why. I think she gets tired of eating pasta constantly, unlike me.

April 29

This morning we were thrilled to awaken to the fact that it was a long weekend, as Monday was a bank holiday. However, although we wanted nothing more than to loll around at home playing with the kids or simply stagnate and watch them jump on the trampoline for hours, I had an event this evening that had been in the diary for a while.

I did a number of these events last year to promote my book *Taste*. They are a straightforward question-and-answer format divided into two forty-five-minute halves. Someone, a well-known, patient journalist or author, asks me questions about the book and my career, and I answer them as best I can without embarrassing myself. The second half is open to questions from the audience.

Some of these events we did last year, at the Coliseum and the Palladium in LA, were designated as fundraisers for War Child, a charity that aids children who are victims of war all over the world, and raised more than £100,000 for its coffers. Today's event, generously hosted by my dear friend Hayley Atwell, was at Royal Albert Hall and was a fundraiser for the Trussell Trust, a charity I've been involved with for a while. I feel the need to write about this, as it sits within a part of the food world that so many of us know little or nothing about but is of enormous significance.

Having been on the board of the Food Bank for New York City for many years, when I moved to England, I was looking to find a similar charity, and the Trussell Trust fit the bill. It oversees more than five hundred food banks in Great Britain and needs money now more than ever, as the number of people requiring their services has increased by 40 percent in the last year alone. The cost of the most basic necessities, especially fuel and food, has skyrocketed as the standard of living has fallen.

How strange that we have never been able to grow food on such a scale or transport it as quickly as we can today, and yet food insecurity is growing. This is not the case only in impoverished nations or war-torn countries, but also in some of the wealthiest countries in the world, including the UK. Hence my doing the event, which tonight raised over £100,000 for the Trussell Trust. I was glad that my older children Isabel and Nicolo were there. I do wonder how strange it must be to see your father onstage or in films. For actors it's just a job, but fame means so much to society, especially nowadays, that it can be very off-putting to those in the famous person's orbit. But it seems that they are used to it now and are actually very protective of me when we are out in public, which I greatly appreciate. But in the end, I really just want what every parent wants, which is for them to feel proud of me.

I will now guiltily recount the dinner we had this evening after that altruistic event. It took place in a little Greek restaurant, which was new to us all, called Suzi Tros.

The creamiest yogurt with dill was served first, along with thick, perfectly baked oily focaccia, followed by a rich *taramasalata*, sea bass carpaccio with a hint of jalapeño, and plates of tuna tartare.

I avoided the spicier servings of meatballs and roasted eggplant that came next. However, as I had gorged on the first four plates, while I sipped a minerally white from Crete, I was well sated.

April 30

For the children's dinner we made chicken cutlets, white rice, and steamed Romanesco, a pointy, green broccoli-like vegetable. Felicity and I had pork belly, which she expertly prepared, tended to, and cooked. The cracklin' was as addictive as that word without the "lin'." The meat was so moist that even *I* didn't struggle to eat it. Served with a potato salad, coleslaw from the farmers' market, and a couple of glasses of French red, it was delicious.

I love sitting down to eat with my family. I remember my father telling me that when he came home from work, he looked forward to us all sitting down to dinner together even when we were moody teenagers. I felt the same with my moody teenagers (most of the time), and I feel the same now with the younger kids. The difficulty is that our lives are much more hectic than my parents' lives were. Because both my parents worked in a nearby high school, as my sisters and I got older and had after-school activities, they were always home before us, and when we arrived the table was set and dinner was promptly served. But often Felicity and I will have work-related events or dinners in the evening or late afternoons that preclude us from eating with Matteo and Millie, and a lot of my professional commitments require me to travel or work strange hours. We usually feed the kids by six or six thirty p.m. because they're hungry and we need to get them to bed in good time, which often can take quite a while, as every parent knows. Teeth need to be brushed; stories read; attempts to empty bladders and bowels followed through with, no matter what the outcome; songs sung; and questions answered, such as:

"How much older are you than Mummy?"

"Twenty-one years."

"Then why is she taller?"

And so on.

To be fair, Felicity will eat earlier with the children when she is at home, but I still have difficulty doing so even though I know it's better for you. (Are the Spanish really unhealthy then, because they start eating at like ten p.m. on a good night?) But so many Brits and Americans feed their kids quite early. I picked up Millie at about five p.m. from a playdate a month ago and she told me she'd just finished dinner. Which means she ate at four thirty p.m. I had no idea her friend lived in a retirement home.

Anyway, because we have indulged our children a bit, they have a limited number of dishes they will eat, although Matteo is branching out, thank God, so often we will make something for them and then a different meal for us, which we will eat after they are in bed. More work? Yes. Worth it? Sometimes. Truth be told, I really am looking forward to someday not having to cook two different meals and eating at a reasonable hour. All of us. Together.

May 1

Soba noodles in homemade chicken broth with chopped chives, wild garlic leaves, and scallions was our post-workout early lunch. I attempted to poach an egg in mine to make it like an egg-drop soup, but it didn't work out very well. It still tasted good, but I must learn how to properly make my eggs drop.

This afternoon I made jam sandwiches for the kids with spears of cucumber and carrots to assuage my guilt about making them nothing healthier than jam sandwiches. But since they each had a friend over, I figured that jam sandwiches were a safe bet for four kids. Luckily, I was right.

After cleaning up the leftover crusts of the jam sandwiches and the uneaten carrots and cucumber spears that I'd slaved over, I opened the fridge drawer and was confronted with four beautiful eggplants. "What to do with them?" wondered I.

I sliced two of them lengthwise, medium thickness; slathered them in olive oil and sprinkled them with oregano and salt; and put them under the grill ("broiler" if you're American), flipping them occasionally, for about twenty minutes. I had seen Nigella Lawson prepare them this way and was inspired. I sliced the remaining two eggplants the same way and grilled them with olive oil, garlic, cherry tomatoes, red onion, and salt. Felicity and I ate both versions with pieces of a warm baguette standing at the counter as a midafternoon snack. Next time I must remember to add goat cheese.

* * *

The kids' friends left around cocktail hour, so I decided to make one. Not a kid, a cocktail. I thought about a Vesper martini. Then I thought again.

Instead, at Felicity's suggestion I made a Paloma, a drink that she'd recently tasted. Gin, grapefruit juice, lime juice, and agave, all shaken and served over rocks with a big splash of sparkling water. It's supposed to be made with tequila, but I prefer the gin version. Very refreshing. Here is one way to make it:

Paloma

Salt
2 ounces Tanqueray No. Ten
2 ounces fresh grapefruit juice
½ ounce fresh lime juice
½ ounce simple syrup
Ice
3 to 4 ounces cold San Pellegrino
1 grapefruit and/or lime wedge, for serving

- Rim a cocktail glass with salt.
- Pour all the ingredients except the San Pellegrino into a cocktail shaker filled with ice.
- Shake for about 30 seconds or so.
- Strain it into the cocktail glass.
- Add San Pellegrino to taste.

- Garnish with the wedge of grapefruit or lime or both.
- Give it someone you love (who is of drinking age) during the summer months.
- Then make one for yourself.

At night I made a piece of filet steak, some leftover star pasta with butter and cheese, and a side of peas for the kids. They ate very well.

After they were in bed, Felicity ate the rest of the filet steak and a salad. I mixed both versions of the remaining eggplant, cut them into bite-size pieces, and tossed them in a pan with some fresh basil while I boiled some penne rigate. Reserving some of the pasta water (always), I strained the pasta, put a large helping into the pan with the eggplant, added a bit of pasta water to emulsify it, turned off the heat, grated Parmigiano over the top, and tossed it some more. At the last minute I added a dollop of creamy goat cheese. It was a sort of version of the Sicilian dish *pasta alla Norma*, and it was quite nice. I must try to re-create it one day. But I do worry that as often happens, the next attempt will be overthought and won't turn out as well. It's like the second performance of a play that's gone well on opening night. Any attempt to repeat the same performance fails dismally because it's an idea of a memory.

Before retiring to bed, Felicity and I watched a crime drama (are there any other kinds of dramas these days?) on a streamer in which most of the actors were good but most of the writing was not.

May 2

During my workout I kept thinking about eggs and how I was going to prepare some for breakfast when I finished. The egg. In Latin, *ovum*. The egg is always on my mind. I love it. Them. I love the shape of them, and I really love to eat them. In any form. Fried, scrambled, poached, soft-boiled, hard-boiled, as a Spanish tortilla, as a frittata, as an omelet, scotched, coddled, "quiched," dropped, and so on. They are practically the perfect food. My father always wanted to write a cookbook about eggs because he loves them so much. On Saturday mornings, when weather allowed, he would set up his Coleman two-burner camping stove on our back patio and make fried eggs in the out-of-doors. He said they tasted better. His cry of "*Who wants eggs?!*" in his strong baritone would echo across our property. I was first in line. And he was right; the eggs did taste better. Everything does when it's cooked outside. Why is that?

Sometimes I go to YouTube and watch Jacques Pépin make an omelet just because it's so beautiful to watch him do it even though he's cooking it indoors. He makes it look so easy and I can imagine just how good it tastes. I wish I could make an omelet like Jacques Pépin. I wish I could make *anything* like Jacques Pépin. In short, I really love eggs. And Jacques Pépin.

I also love egg cups.

May 4

After rising a bit earlier than usual because I wanted to exercise before a couple of meetings in Soho, I readied the kids' breakfasts and school snacks while Felicity got them dressed. Matteo ate a bowl of organic but obscenely sweet cereal, and Millie ate some yogurt. I had an orange juice and a double espresso as always. After my workout I had only a few bites of a banana as I was running late.

When my meetings were finished around noon, I realized I was famished. I also realized I was directly across the street from Tonkotsu, a ramen joint that I love. I entered and thankfully was given the menu right away. The place was empty save for one customer who I could tell recognized me but was unsure from where, because he just kept staring at me. To catch my attention, he suggested I order the Tokyo Ramen because it was good. I told him I knew that, which was a lie, and thanked him. However, I really wanted to try it, because it was chicken-broth based, not pork-broth based (I always find pork broth too salty) but still contained the fatty, soft pieces of pork and of course noodles. However, because the fellow had suggested it, I was *afraid* to order it, because it might seem like I was opening the door to engage with him, thus unleashing a battery of questions about how he might know me. I was paralyzed for a moment. But I *really* wanted it, so I ordered it, and my prophecy came true.

As I waited for the ramen to arrive, the confused fellow continued his unblinking stare, then finally asked me how he knew me, then suddenly realized that I was an actor but said he couldn't remember which films I had been in, and then asked me how I liked England, and I told him I liked it just fine, and then he told me something about his ex-girlfriend and movies he likes, but I couldn't concentrate on chatting with him because I was so hungry and was also attempting to respond to a couple of neglected emails. I was doing my best not to be rude, but I just didn't want to have the conversation I have had many times, which goes something like this:

PERSON: How do I know you?

ME: I don't know.

PERSON: Are you in the . . . pharmaceutical industry?

ME: No.

PERSON: Are you sure?

ME: Very.

PERSON: But I know . . . I know . . . wait, are you someone famous?

ME: Um, well—

PERSON: Are you that weatherman?

ME: No. [relenting] I'm an actor.

PERSON: Oh! . . . Yeah. What show are you on?

ME: I'm not on a show.

PERSON: But I've seen you on TV.

ME: Probably.

PERSON: In what?

ME: I don't know.

PERSON: Films?!

ME: Yes.

PERSON: Which ones?

ME: I've done a lot.

PERSON: Like what?

[I NAME A FILM.]

PERSON: No, that's not it.

ME: Well, like I said, I've done—

PERSON: What's your name?

[I TELL THEM. THEY THINK.]

PERSON: Hmm . . . tell me another film.

At this point I usually excuse myself politely or suggest they Google me.

Basically, whenever I am dining out, that's the scenario. Either that, or people know me so well they tell me things about me that even *I* don't know. Anyway, as the fellow left, the ramen came, and it was even better than I'd anticipated it would be. With some edamame and a small, cold sake, I was very comforted.

For dinner I made a sauce with fresh tomatoes, onions, garlic, and basil to serve over some homemade spinach pasta that Felicity had made a couple of weeks before and we had tucked away in the freezer. But when she arrived home, we had a bit of a tiff and neither of us ate. I returned the still-frozen pasta to the freezer and put the sauce in Tupperware in the fridge. I hate it when that happens. Both the argument and the forgoing of a meal. I blame myself. Partly. Mostly.

May 5

The alarm went off at four thirty a.m. We were leaving for Bordeaux for a three-day holiday. It was the king's coronation, so we decided to show our support by visiting the land of the monarchy's centuries-old rival. Felicity, wisely as ever, booked a place on the coast. It was a large house that had been converted into a boutique hotel called Villa La Tosca, and though it was nothing fancy or expensive, it was lovely, and the staff were very welcoming. I had never been to Bordeaux before and was thrilled to be there.

After we wandered the small property for a bit and the kids found tadpoles in the little man-made stream that was fed by the overflow from the freshwater pool (great design, especially for kids), we sat down to a lunch the hotel had prepared. A platter of *fruits de mer* consisting of oysters, shrimp, pink and brown cockles, langoustines, and whelks sat on the table surrounded by boards of various cured meats, cheeses, and homemade compotes; two baguettes; a bowl of lightly dressed salad; and a bottle of white wine. Probably one of the best lunches I have ever had in France. Truly.

We had dinner at a casual fish place right on the bay that had more than just fish. More oysters, of course; a delicious fish soup; great foie gras; salmon tartare (too many sesame seeds); and something else I can't remember. A bottle of local white went well with it all.

Millie and Matteo had steak and pan-fried fish, respectively, with a side of plain pasta. Matteo actually ate his fish. He has made a point recently of trying new foods of his own volition. I think he's inspired by the cooking class he takes once a week at school. Last week he made "Greek pasta salad" with penne, cucumber, tomatoes, peppers, feta cheese, and olive oil but stopped short of putting olives in his. He said he doesn't like them, or maybe he just didn't want it to be *too* Greek.

Since we've arrived in France Matteo has been very adventurous when it comes to food. Of course, he keeps reminding us of this as he counts and *re*counts aloud how many different foods he has tried in his only two meals so far and then asks us how many different foods *we* have counted that he has tried, and then no matter what number we say, he ups it by one or two. Then he eats some more. Then he begins the counting/recounting again. His boasting and numerical obsession notwithstanding, I am very proud of him. He'll be the best-fed human abacus the world has ever known.

May 6

Breakfast on the balcony of the room that we are sharing with the kids. The usual French breakfast fare. The best baguette ever in the history of baguettes.

We went for lunch at an oyster shack in a long line of oyster shacks on the bay of a nearby town. Shrimp, clams, oysters, pâté, and bread, which is basically the whole menu. Millie ate the bread. Matteo ate the shrimp. Fee and I ate it all. And some white wine. Everything was just . . . okay. Would I go again? No.

The manager of our hotel, Aurelien, who had given us a lift to the town, came to pick us up and drove us back to the hotel. We chatted in both directions about food, and from the sound of it Aurelien is quite the cook, having grown up in a family of professional cooks. As we were heading back to the hotel he asked if we were interested in going to a farmers' market the next day to buy some produce and cook together. Felicity and I jumped at the chance. Which is difficult to do in a small car.

In the evening we walked about ten minutes to what seemed like a fairly new, characterless place that had good food. I can't remember what Felicity had for an appetizer, but I had the ravioli, which were accompanied by tiny morels in too much cream but were nonetheless delicious. For the entrées Felicity had scallops, lightly seared, and I had the *boudin blanc*, which was good if a bit bland. The vegetables, mangetout and some string beans, were a kind of sad afterthought. The frites were amazing, however. Millie devoured her steak and Matteo peeled the skin off his *boudin blanc* (another brave order for him, of which he reminded us) and stuffed the meat between two pieces of baguette.

May 7

Aurelien drove us to the farmers' market about twenty minutes away. It was not huge or varied, but the produce was fresh and local. We bought duck breast for a carpaccio he was going to make, a shallot, parsley, tomatoes, lettuce, chipolatas for the kids, and rabbit pâté for us. I wanted to buy more of everything and then some. Felicity and I tend to overbuy at farmers' markets, but having grown up in restaurants, Aurelien is not one to waste food and kept looking at me askance whenever I suggested another purchase. Finally, when I proposed buying an entire rabbit and he shook his head like a disappointed parent, I knew it was time to leave.

We didn't buy seafood there because Aurelien didn't like the look of the oysters or anything else, so he called his fishmonger near the hotel and placed an order with him.

In twenty minutes, we were in the little *poissonnerie*, where a lanky, all-too-handsome fishmonger in his thirties welcomed us. Aurelien and he are the best of friends, as was proven when Aurelien walked behind the counter like he owned the joint and chastised the young fellow for not having the oysters he'd asked for. He did, however, have the cooked crabs and some langoustines. After tasting two different tartares (dorade and tuna, dressed with olive oil, salt, and chives), we bought two small containers of those as well as a large piece of cod with panko breadcrumbs that we thought would make a good dinner for the kids. Aurelien felt it was overkill and was not pleased. I know because when we asked for them, I saw him wince.

Still bereft of oysters, we drove about three minutes down the road to an oyster shack and bought two dozen number 2s and two dozen number 4s. Oyster size is classified by numbers, 00 being the largest, 5 being the smallest. I don't know why, and I don't care. Anyway, for a very reasonable number of euros, we bought forty-eight oysters for three adults. To buy that many of such high quality in London, one would have to take out a loan.

When we returned to the hotel, the kids ran to the small stream and searched for more tadpoles as we donned aprons and began to cook. I started the kids' sausages and Aurelien showed us how to make his simple fresh mayonnaise.

Aurelien's Mayonnaise

1 egg yolk, beaten with a tablespoon of Dijon mustard
Sunflower oil, drizzled in slowly while you continue to beat until the mixture becomes thick and you can create peaks
Salt, pepper, and a squeeze of lemon to taste

He also opened all the oysters because his shucking knives were basically small daggers, and we were both too afraid to use them. Felicity washed the lettuce, and I gave the kids their sausages, then chopped the parsley and the shallot for the butter mixture that would go onto the larger oysters, which would then be topped with breadcrumbs and placed under the broiler/grill for six minutes.

Aurelien finished arranging the raw oysters, langoustine, and crab on a large silver platter, punctuating it all with slices of lemon. I topped the large oysters with the shallot-butter mixture and the breadcrumbs, then slid them into the oven. Aurelien had also made a salad dressing of olive oil, balsamic vinegar, salt, pepper, and honey.

When the tops of the oysters were golden brown, we whisked them straight to the table on the porch off the kitchen, where everything else had been set along with more wine and bread. Here the three of us ate our seafood feast looking out at the sea, and except for half a crab and three oysters, we ate everything. All of it was delicious, especially Aurelien's cooked oysters. Jesus. WTF?! *Quelle révélation!!*

I indulged so much that I needed a double espresso to continue functioning this afternoon.

May 8

Croissants, juice, baguette, and coffee for breakfast before leaving the hotel. We had nothing much to eat on the plane for obvious reasons.

At home in the late morning, I made a light tomato sauce to use for a few different dishes over the next couple of days. Also made cannellini beans with chopped carrot, onion, celery, and sliced garlic. Boiled some thin small pasta. While that cooked, we gave the kids salami, tomatoes, cucumbers, carrots, and a baguette for lunch. After pureeing half of the bean mixture and returning it to the pot, I tossed it and some of the tomato sauce with the pasta for my lunch.

I like to make tomato sauce whenever I return home after a trip, or when I arrive at a vacation home or wherever I'm staying while filming. I find it grounding. After the sauce has cooked for even just a few minutes, the new space smells more like a home. Obviously, I love going to restaurants, trying different dishes or old staples in the hands of a new chef, but I know that after a few too many meals out in a row I long to be home so I can eat what I want to eat when I want to eat it. And besides all that, I miss the actual *act* of cooking. Choosing the recipes, finding the produce, prepping it, cooking it, serving it, and eating it. The satisfaction and joy that those simple acts bring is made even greater when what is served is shared. Sharing food is one of the purest human acts.

* * *

Tonight I made pasta with butter and cheese for the kids with a side of broccoli and green beans, as they barely ate vegetables all weekend. Spying a packet of cod in the fridge that was about to go off, I decided to make it, *alla livornese*. Here's how I did it:

Cod alla Livornese

Salt
About 1 pound skinless cod (enough for 2 people)
Extra-virgin olive oil
Half an onion, chopped
2 garlic cloves, halved
12 pomodorini (small tomatoes), coarsely chopped
4 basil leaves, torn up a bit
1 cup white wine
About 8 black or green olives (or a mix of both), unseasoned
1 tablespoon capers, rinsed

- Lightly salt the piece of cod and set aside.
- In a medium pan, heat a glug of olive oil over medium heat. Add the onion and garlic and sauté until soft, then add the tomatoes, basil, and some salt. Cook until a sauce of sorts has formed.
- Increase the heat to high, add the wine, and let the alcohol burn off. Reduce the heat to a simmer and add the olives and capers. Add the cod to the center of the pan, spooning some of the tomato mixture over it. Cover the pan. Cook for about 5 minutes, then flip the fish and cover again, cooking for about 3 minutes. The fish

should be opaque in the middle and warm. Serve covered with the sauce and drizzled with a little extra-virgin olive oil.

We served some lightly poached asparagus on the side. The whole thing took about fifteen minutes, and I must admit it was good.

May 9

Lunch was just picking at things in between Zoom meetings.

Felicity was out this evening. She said it was work related. I chose to believe her.

I made chipolata sausages for the kids in the new air fryer (amazing contraption) and a side of rice and peas, and that was that.

After I put them to bed, I made conchiglie pasta (large shells) with minced onion, garlic, fennel, fennel seeds, ground Italian sausage, and the tomato sauce I had made on Monday. I sautéed all of that in a pan and tossed it with the pasta and some cheese. I had three helpings at nine p.m. Not wise but delicious.

May 10

I ate no breakfast as I had a PET scan with radioactive contrast this morning, so I had to abstain from eating or drinking anything except water until after the scan. I have them about every six months because I was treated for throat cancer five years ago but still need to be checked. It's always a little nerve-racking, having the scans. One hopes against hope that the results will be negative, which means positive in the world of diagnoses. Which means you can relax. At least for a while. After being misdiagnosed for two years and delaying scans, I am hyper-vigilant now. Although the cancer was only at the base of my tongue and had not metastasized, I insist on getting full-body scans, not just head and neck scans, regularly. Better safe than sorry. Seven years ago, I wasn't safe, and I was very sorry.

Knowing many people who have died of cancer and having had it myself, the fear of it is still very present, but my experience and knowledge have allowed me to give others support and advice from time to time. They have also steeled me for the next battle, should it come. I guess sometimes you must be made extremely weak to find a strength you never knew you had.

The scan took quite a while, and I was famished afterward. I wandered around Marylebone High Street looking for a place to eat, but many of them were in between breakfast and lunch, so I ended up in a restaurant I used go to a lot when a friend owned it. I wouldn't have gone in normally, out of loyalty, but I was famished. I ordered the chicken liver appetizer, which came on a piece of toasted baguette with chopped egg, cucumber, and dill and was delicious.

Asparagus with a soft-boiled egg was my second dish. There were both white and green asparagus, which were all a bit sad and wizened. The white ones were so old that they were fibrous and inedible, and the green ones were on the cusp of woody but palatable. What a shame, because I just saw the most gorgeous bunches of asparagus in France a few days ago that I didn't buy because I thought Aurelien would be miffed. A beetroot salad, both gold and red with some lettuce and squares of toasted goat cheese in a light olive oil dressing with fresh peas and pea shoots, came next. It was good, but if the goat cheese had been warm, it would have been ten times better. Besides the appetizer it all felt like it had been waiting in the fridge or the larder for too long before it was assembled and finally served. But as I was starving, I ate it all and washed it down with a lager.

I napped this afternoon because the tracer they injected me with for the scan made me feel a bit ill. After an hour's kip and an espresso, I felt better.

I took my eldest son, Nicolo, to St. John tonight. It is one of several restaurants owned and run by Fergus Henderson. The original St. John opened in 1994 and ushered in a new wave of British cooking. It's all about meat. Lots of it and all of it. Nose-to-tail cooking. As little as possible goes to waste. They are not a chain of restaurants because, although every one of them has a rustic urban aesthetic—white walls, simple wooden tables, exposed pipes, and paper or large chalkboard menus—the dishes of the day differ slightly. This night we went to a new, small iteration in Marylebone.

I had a glass of sharp white as I waited for Nicolo, who arrived soon afterward. Nico is training to be a chef at Leiths culinary school in London after graduating from the University of Sussex with a degree in politics. (I am not going to pretend I wasn't thrilled when he told me he wanted to be a chef instead of a politician.) He did incredibly well at university but is excelling at Leiths. In short, he was born to do it. He has the innate talent as well as the imagination, drive, and exacting nature to be a great chef. And he's handsome. And he's a nice fella to boot. I'll stop bragging now. This is what we ate:

Deep-fried Welsh rarebit

Middle-White pork belly with mustard

Anchovy toast and parsley salad

Lemon sole with tartar sauce

Calf's liver with braised chicory and pickled walnut

Wedge salad

A bottle of Chablis

It was all incredible. Incredible.

After our meal we parted ways, Nico back to the flat he shares with his twin sister, Isabel, and a friend of theirs, and me back home. They are no longer living in our house and, barring anything disastrous, may never do so again. I know it's clichéd, but it does feel like only yesterday that I held them both, one in each arm, rocked them, sang to them, watched them smile slightly and fall asleep.

* * *

Time is passing too quickly now. I had always heard people who are my age say those words, but I never really understood what they meant. Now I do.

The slower one becomes, the faster time moves. How? Why? Is it because we finally understand time and are now able to gauge how long we've got left? At the age of sixty-three I probably have another twenty years, thirty if I'm very lucky. But now, as opposed to when I was younger, I *know* what twenty years is. I *know* what thirty years is. They are nothing. Just a glimpse of life. So, one panics. Or I do. Therefore, I think of death often. Very often. Too often perhaps.

But I come by it honestly. Thoughts of death, my own and others', have always been very present in my mind, since before Kate or I got ill. Death was very much a part of my upbringing, not only because it's a well-discussed subject in southern Italian culture but also because my father's father was a stonecutter who owned his own monument business. Death was doubly present.

My father, an artist, and my uncle, an architect, often designed gravestones for the monument business, Stanley Tucci and Sons. Most Sundays of my childhood were spent in the Peekskill cemetery, where so many of the monuments they worked on over decades still stood. The Tucci family monument, designed by my father, was among them, and we would visit it regularly to pay our respects to my paternal grandmother, who lay alongside the two-year-old daughter she'd lost and another young relative who had died only days after being born. As time passed, my grandfather took his place there, as did uncles and aunts, and someday my parents will find their way into that same soil. The plot was designed to hold many members of the Tucci clan. Death with great forethought. I'm honored that my name will be chiseled into that granite as well, but I hope someone also plants a tree for me somewhere. An olive tree. Olive trees have so much to offer, and I'd like to be somewhat useful even in death.

May 11

Half a banana, orange juice, and a double espresso for breakfast before a weight workout with our trainer Daryll Martin.

Gnawed on half a croissant, appropriately, watching Matteo's French assembly, in which all the kids were dressed as animals and sang songs in French about the animals they were dressed as. (What a terrible sentence that just was.) Matteo was dressed in a two-piece alligator costume. When the jaws of the headpiece were open, his head was visible, and therefore he was able to see. The problem was that the jaws kept closing every time he moved. This made his head seem like it was being consumed by the alligator. Eventually his teacher plucked it off him so he could sing and see freely. I felt so bad for him, but I couldn't help but laugh. Afterward many parents told me that it was the best part of the show. I was so proud.

After a long meeting with BBC Studios about the next phase of *Stan Is Still Searching for Italy* or whatever, Lottie and I were both starving, so we went to a nearby Italian place we know.

Boiled-then-grilled artichokes, meatballs with a tomato sauce, ricotta with lemon oil, and a hint of black truffle and grilled focaccia were the appetizers we ordered. None of it was particularly good and the focaccia was actually gross. It was toasted on what couldn't have been a very clean grill or griddle because it tasted like someone had run it over with a burning car. My pappardelle with peas and pancetta made me feel a bit ill afterward, as it was heavy and tasted like it had been made with margarine instead of butter. Lottie ordered a small pizza and a salad, both of which she barely ate.

In the end, a terrible waste of food and money. And the service was slow. Very. So, time was wasted as well. I don't mean to complain, but if one is paying a lot for a meal, it should be good food served efficiently, and that's that.

This evening there was a dinner in a hotel restaurant for about sixty people in the film business that we had been invited to. The food was fucking awful. I had one bite of something and never ate the rest of the night. Felicity did eat and had diarrhea the next morning.

May 12

Oatmeal for breakfast with honey and almond milk.

Walked kids to school.

Did a thirty-minute Pilates class.

Reread the entry I wrote about St. John and got hungry, so I had to go and eat. Made scrambled eggs with leftover rice and peas and some scallions. A bad version of egg fried rice. Really bad, in fact.

Felt annoyed with myself that I hadn't prepared it properly. Then I noticed that Lottie had ordered some bagels, tuna salad, and scallion cream cheese from some new place in London. The owner is from NYC, so it was all supposed to be authentic.

It was.

I toasted half a bagel, then cut it in half again. On one quarter I put a dollop of tuna and some lettuce, and on the other a dollop of cream cheese. Best Jewish deli food I've had since I moved here ten years ago.

Much better than my inauthentic egg fried rice.

Got hungry midafternoon. Had a few *pomodorini* with feta cheese, olive oil, and basil on mini toasted crackers and a half a nonalcoholic beer. I like to have the flavor of wine or beer along with water with a meal, but during the day I don't want the alcohol. There are some pretty good nonalcoholic beers out there.

* * *

Dinner at Riva with Richard Curtis and Emma Freud. Had not seen them for a very long time and good to catch up. Lovely people who are too smart to be friends with the likes of me. As it turns out, Riva was one of Richard's father's favorite restaurants.

Emma drank beer, Richard drank rosé, Felicity drank nothing because her stomach was still off, and I drank white.

Riva will soon celebrate its thirty-third year of business. This is an extraordinary feat for a restaurant. Andrea Riva, who hails from Lombardy, has created battalions of devoted customers since he opened because his food is authentic and seasonal and the ingredients are of the highest quality. His staff is as devoted to him as he is to them. On top of it all he has a great sense of humor; is a great raconteur fluent in French, German, English, and obviously Italian; is incredibly well-read; and is basically a walking encyclopedia of food. A rare person.

This is what we ate:

Starters

Fried zucchini flowers stuffed with mozzarella and anchovies

Fried soft-shell crabs

Carciofi alla giudia with prosciutto on the side

Mains

Richard: Suckling pig (served every day all year round)

Emma: Gnocchi with lemon butter sauce and asparagus

Felicity: The same as Emma

Me: Pappardelle with a meat ragù

Great. All great. I think Richard ate the suckling pig before it hit the table.

May 13

Felicity is still suffering from stomach issues and Matteo's strep throat has resurfaced after less than a week since it disappeared. Millie and I are fine but it's not going to be a fun weekend.

I did a weight workout and then half an hour of yoga with Monique, our Pilates trainer and dear friend. I am more obsessed with exercise than I was before I got sick. Five to six days a week of Pilates, yoga, and weights. Our trainers Monique and Daryll have strengthened my core and increased my aerobic capability and flexibility. During my illness my muscles atrophied, and it has taken quite some time to regain them. Also, if one devotes as much time to one's stomach as I do, it's not a terrible idea to devote even a little bit of time to one's heart and body as well.

Afterward I made a two-egg omelet cooked in a bit of butter and olive oil. I ate it topped with anchovies and sliced tomato on a buttered warm baguette. My God. Really. My God. As I'm writing this, I'm getting hungry again.

Realizing that a lot of the vegetables in the fridge were about to go off (I don't know why I always wait until the eleventh hour of their lives), I made a soup with spring onions, onion, leeks, potatoes, a bit of butter, olive oil, and chicken stock that Felicity had made in our Instant Pot. I puréed it all with an immersion blender, which did a bad job of it. (It has been making a weird sound, so I think it's broken.) With a dash of nutmeg and a little pepper, the soup was good but, as I say, poorly puréed, and I was too lazy to put it into the food processer, so I just stuck it in the fridge as it was.

I gave Millie a lunch of salami, baguette, and tomatoes. I brought Matteo a salami sandwich in his room, where he was despondently listening to an audiobook and still feeling quite a bit under the weather. He loves audiobooks as well as reading. Two very healthy addictions. While the soup was cooking, I made some marinara for myself and had it with some egg tagliolini. I ate it while Millie and I played Dinosaur Guess Who. Then I had an iced espresso while we played a card game called Rat-a-Tat Cat.

This evening I had a speaking engagement at Annabel's, a rather posh club I had never been to. Felicity's sickly stomach prevented her from joining me, so I went alone. (I'm so brave.) It was Annabel's sixtieth anniversary, and they asked me to record a video message for them and answer some questions about the place, and I told them I had never been there before, so I just gave my first impressions, which naturally were positive. I had a scotch at the bar before dinner. I was seated with my interviewer, Donald Sloan, head of the Oxford Cultural Collective, and the lovely British chef and presenter Andi Oliver. They were both great company, and of course we talked a lot about food. The event took place in Matteo's, one of the seven restaurants in the building that houses Annabel's.

The food was delicious. I had a crabmeat appetizer dressed with olive oil and lemon, and eggplant parmigiana for my main. The eggplant parmigiana was made with mozzarella, which I don't usually care for because it makes the dish too heavy, but it was used sparingly and the whole thing was very light.

It was so interesting to note that once again almost the entire staff was Italian, from the bartender to the waiters, the manager, etc. Gracious, knowledgeable, efficient. I know I'm biased but at this point it's becoming clear to me that London restaurants would crumble without them. Such an interesting decision, Brexit. One can only ask, whose foot were they aiming for?

When the event ended, I was led through the byzantine building and came to an opulent bar made of alabaster and glass, or something in between the two, that was half a football pitch long. Every other room in the building had been teeming with people, but here there was no one save a young couple and a lone bartender. The couple left a moment later. As I waited for my taxi, I couldn't give up the opportunity to have a quiet drink alone in such unusual and ornate surroundings. So, I did. Forty-five minutes later I was lying next to my ailing wife as my children snored the comically loud snores of the innocent and guilt-free.

May 14

Felicity and Matteo are both on the mend, and the sun showed its shy self. We sat in the garden and read a bit, meaning Felicity read an entire book and I looked at Pinterest while the kids jumped on the trampoline. I wrangled four fading zucchini from the fridge, sliced them into rounds, coated them with olive oil and salt, and placed them in the oven to roast for about twenty minutes.

I fried up some sliced potatoes in a cast-iron pan, then layered the whole lot in a small baking tin with the previous day's marinara and some grated Parmigiano and baked it for about thirty minutes. This is the way my father's family made eggplant parmigiana but this time I just made it without the eggplant.

Full disclosure: I am writing this at 10:05 a.m. the next day. I just ate the zucchini parmigiana on a warm baguette for breakfast. I had to stop myself from eating all of it. My repertoire is limited, but I must admit that the dishes I do make are pretty good. However, I did burn the potatoes a bit in my rush to cook them quickly. Impatience.

In so many attempts to save time, so many other things are wasted.

In the afternoon we used the leftover chicken meat from Felicity's stock to make a chicken salad. I tried to replicate Aurelien's mayo but the sunflower oil I used was so potent that it tasted dreadful, and I had to dump it, which was frustrating because I'd practically torn a rotator cuff whisking the goddamn stuff.

Defaulting to Hellmann's, which I actually love, I mixed it into the chopped chicken with some finely diced celery and chives. Felicity and I ate it on little toasted crackers we had brought from France topped with slices of cucumber.

Why is chicken salad so comforting? Tuna salad as well. I get cravings all the time for a tuna sandwich, with lettuce on toasted rye, from a Manhattan coffee shop. I must have eaten hundreds of them over the two decades I spent in that town. Paired with a bowl of soup, it's a very hearty and affordable meal. As I write this, all I want is one of those sandwiches, and sadly that's not going to happen. I used to walk practically the length and breadth of Manhattan almost every week when I found myself jobless, which was quite often. I would visit galleries, museums, and bookshops, or just wander through neighborhoods taking in the architecture of old New York, which new development gnawed away at year by year. My youthful ramblings were sustained by bowls of soup (chicken noodle, split pea) and sandwiches (BLT, turkey club, chicken salad, and of course tuna) eaten in old coffee shops that themselves have since fallen victim to "progress."

What's the first food memory we have? I don't have one. Does anyone? Obviously, we're just babies when we first breastfeed, first slurp soft food, and first chew solid food, but no one I've ever met has a memory that stretches back that far. Yet even as we mature and become capable of eating more and more things, how many people can tell you they remember the very first time they ate pasta or steak or fish, and whether they liked it or not? When did you first realize you liked salmon? Or a hamburger? Or French fries? Or a tomato? Or basil? No one remembers. We just know that we like them, and so we eat them. We are more likely to remember why we *don't* like certain things, but this usually happens when we try something new as an adult. But the reasons for not liking certain flavors since childhood are usually unclear. (Unless one came from a household of lousy cooks, which creates confused palates and unreasonable dislikes, in which case the reason is very clear: everything just tasted awful.) But basically, like or dislike, most of us don't remember our very first taste.

It's like the realization that we are mortal. Tom Stoppard wrote in his brilliant play *Rosencrantz and Guildenstern Are Dead*, "Whatever became of the moment when one first knew about death? There must have been one, a moment, in childhood, when it first occurred to you that you don't go on forever. It must have been shattering, stamped into one's memory. And yet I can't remember it."

A few hours later I ate some of the potato-leek soup straight from the fridge. It was nice and chilled and perfect for a hot day. However, little strands of leeks and onions kept getting stuck in my teeth because I hadn't puréed it properly, but I wasn't about to start now. Why? Impatience.

That evening Felicity sautéed some scallops, but they didn't really sear because the pan had not gotten hot enough, which was my fault because I had reduced the heat, as the butter was about to burn, and didn't communicate that. They didn't work out as well as she had hoped. She ate a few, but as I had overindulged in cold soup not long before, I had only one. We stashed the rest in the fridge. Afterward we watched *Colin from Accounts*, a brilliant Australian half-hour comedy. It alleviated all sadness caused by the underseared scallops.

May 15

After seeing the kids off to school and exercising, I made myself scrambled eggs and avocado with sliced tomato. Luckily it was a tomato that actually *tasted like a tomato*. Like so many vegetables these days, tomatoes often taste of nothing. When did that start happening? Things used to taste like what they were. Now something that looks like a tomato or a carrot tastes like just a *thought* of those things. If fruit and vegetables are organic, they usually taste better, but not always. I remember pulling carrots out of my grandfather's garden and the depth of flavor being profound. It was the same with everything he grew, from onions to plums. Anyway, I ate the egg-avocado-tomato combo on a small, warm tortilla. I actually ate two. They were delicious.

This week was going to busy, with a podcast and Zoom meetings and two events for the Prince's Trust. I had been asked to present an award, along with our friend Holly Willoughby, to one of the winners. It was a huge event at the Theatre Royal with a champagne reception beforehand. I had no idea that the scope of the charity was as far-reaching as it is. Since it started in 1976, the Prince's Trust has helped over a million people access schooling, counseling, and housing and train for their first or new career. This event was to honor some of those shining examples of personal achievement who had benefited from the trust. Holly and I presented the Young Change Maker Award to a young man named Motaz, an asylum seeker from Yemen. Only a year after he found refuge in Belfast along with his family, he is fluent in English, excelling in his studies, volunteering to help others through the trust, and on his way to fulfilling his dream of being a dentist. He's only seventeen years of age and has endured more hardship in his short life than I will ever know. I was in awe.

I had to leave after I presented to get home in time for a call, and because the traffic was so horrible, I walked across Waterloo Bridge and caught the train home. I was quite hungry but didn't want to eat a lot because I wanted to save myself for dinner, so I stopped at an upscale chain place, which shall remain nameless, in South Bank and ordered a ham and cheese toastie on a focaccia-like bread. The ingredients were good, except for some sort of creamy spread on the inside. I think it might have been *besciamella* but I can't be sure. I can be sure, however, of the fact that it was disgusting. I took three bites and hopped on the train feeling I had taken three bites too many.

May 16

This morning I was getting the kids ready and seeing them off to school on my own as Felicity had to catch a train to the Cotswolds to visit the set of a TV adaptation of her client Jilly Cooper's book *Rivals*. I would be leaving in a couple of hours by taxi, bound for the event at Buckingham Palace for the prior day's Prince's Trust honorees and those of us who had presented to them. I was excited and of course a bit nervous, and at the same time found the dichotomy of my life ironic.

Before I hobnob at the palace, here I am scrubbing pots and pans, and wrangling a five-year-old in an attempt to squeeze her into a school uniform while her eight-year-old brother wanders around the kitchen half-undressed, face smeared with jam, repeatedly asking me to watch him throw a tiny javelin he's fashioned out of a stick, a small stone, and some tape.

School mornings are fascinating *Groundhog Day*–like events. My children act as if neither of them has *ever* been to school. It's as though every morning is their *very first morning* of their *very first day* of their *very first year* of their education. They also behave like they have never donned clothes and lost their hearing while they slept, because all our questions, requests, and pleas go unanswered. Old chestnuts such as the following simply evaporate into the ether.

"Can you brush your teeth?"

No response.

"Please put your socks on."

Nothing.

"Where is your jumper?"

Silence.

"What would you like for your snack?"

A long yawn.

"Could you please finish your orange juice?"

A small ball is kicked.

"Please sit down and eat that."

A cup of orange juice is spilled.

Here I was about to meet the newly crowned king of England at an intimate gathering and this was how I was spending my morning. From the mundane to the monarchy in a matter of minutes.

After more of this redundant lunacy, Felicity breezed downstairs beautifully made up, coiffed, and smelling of jasmine or something all too alluring, kissed the kids, and muttered a brisk goodbye that I just barely heard over the sound of my scouring. She obviously must have forgotten that I was to rub shoulders with royalty this morning, because her only words to me were, "Can you strain that broth I made last night?"

As the front door slammed I prayed for her train to be delayed.

For the palace event I had chosen to wear a cream-colored linen double-breasted muted-plaid suit, a white shirt, a brown tie, brown socks, and brown shoes. I love clothing as much as I love food and always like to dress not only well, but appropriately for whatever the occasion might be. I loathe the fact that our world has become so casual. So many people wear the same thing for a night out on the town or to the theater that they wear around the house, which most often is a T-shirt and jeans or even sweatpants. When I did some cocktail videos during lockdown for my Instagram, one person commented very excitedly that I was wearing pants and a belt. Let's face it: adults today dress like children. I'm not suggesting that one don a three-piece suit every day, but anything other than shorts, sneakers, and T-shirts plastered with oversize logos or catchphrases like "I used to drink, but that was hours ago," or "Shit I don't have time for" followed by a list of that "shit" would be a step in the right direction.

The event was to take place between noon and two fifteen p.m., and it was made clear by the organizers that only coffee, tea, and biscuits (British for cookies) would be served. We were therefore advised to eat something beforehand as lunch would not be in the offing.

After seeing the children off to school, I exercised and made myself a hearty breakfast of leftover ziti and scrambled eggs with sautéed onions. It wasn't my best, but I ate a lot, as I was afraid of becoming peckish at the palace.

The event was lovely, and Holly and I chatted again with Motaz, who comports himself with such assurance and great humor. Indeed only coffee, tea, and biscuits were served in a large salon where all the winners and presenters mingled while awaiting the king's arrival. When HRH did appear, we all split into our separate groups, Holly and I with Motaz, and waited for King Charles to make his way to us.

I had met HRH when he was a mere prince at a food-related event where he gave a speech about sustainability, global warming, and organic farming, all of which he began promoting years before they were fashionable or even discussed. He was as charming and articulate on that day as he was on this occasion. When he came round to us, he graciously congratulated Motaz; was charmed by Holly, as is everyone; discussed his passion for Italian food with me; and told me he was a fan of *Searching for Italy*. I thanked him, and then he asked how many children I had. I told him I have five, and he said, "Well, they keep you young." And I said, "Do they?" and he laughed heartily. (I could feel a friendship budding.)

When the event ended, I hopped into a cab and headed home to be jeered at and taken advantage of by my children while I cooked yet another meal for them that they might deign to eat. I kept my name tag, printed with the royal seal, pinned to my lapel to impress them, or just as a visual prompt in case they had forgotten my name.

When I arrived home, they weren't impressed at all. And they kept calling me Mummy.

Rabble.

May 18

Found myself in Heathrow yet again en route to Dublin to do some work for Diageo, the liquor company that owns Tanqueray No. Ten, which I promote, and then do a Q and A at the International Literature Festival Dublin.

I had oatmeal in the lounge and some orange juice and a croissant. I tried the tater tot things again and they were crisper this time. I love a potato cooked in any way, shape, or form.

Arriving at the hotel, I ordered poached eggs, toast, and sausage, and it was delicious. Began press interviews related to T10 for a couple of hours.

After the interviews, we headed to a place called Pichet to film a cocktail tasting at the bar with the Irish T10 ambassador, a bartender named Federico (Fede) Riezzo. Obviously, he's not Irish. He's ridiculously Italian. He just lives in Dublin. Christ, they're everywhere.

At Pichet the young bartender made Fede and me a cocktail of house-made vermouth, T10, orange bitters, and a caperberry garnish. I have always avoided caperberries. I guess because those I must have first eaten years ago were overbrined or too acidic, so I gave up on them. But these were soft and delicate with a floral-tasting pulpy center.

The caperberry itself is the fruit of the bush, and capers are the unopened buds of the flowers. Salted or brined, they have been part of the Mediterranean diet for centuries. Wikipedia has just informed me that Pliny the Elder wrote about how both were used to treat maladies of the spleen, liver, and bladder and, when mixed with vinegar, to cure ulcers of the mouth. Who knows what health benefits they might have when coupled with gin and vermouth, but I can attest to feeling like a million bucks after a few sips and a nibble.

The food at Pichet, cooked by Mark Moriarty, was extraordinary. But it was only the first of a total of five amazing meals I would have over the next few days. Felicity came to meet me the next morning, as did our friends Aidan Quinn and his wife, Lizzie Bracco, who were on their way to Cork, where Aidan was to be honored at a film fest. I had not seen them for too long, but after being together for a few minutes it was as though we had never been parted. Luckily Felicity had organized an itinerary of eating for us over the next couple of days, and we dove in wholeheartedly. Although Aidan was born outside of Chicago, he spent a good deal of his childhood in Ireland and has always spoken of it with tremendous fondness and even longing, so being in Dublin with him was a great joy. It was also a great joy to watch him eat. I say this because when we first met almost forty years ago, when he directed me in a one-act play in New York, he had one of the worst diets of anyone I'd ever known. I can't really remember him eating anything other than fried eggs, toast, hamburgers, and steaks very well done, and potatoes in some form or another. No fish, no salads, no veg, and no wine. Only beer and lots of cigarettes. But over the years he wisely—because he is indeed very wise—altered his diet for the better and quit smoking. He became very interested in and knowledgeable about red wine, and although he can still be a bit picky about certain things, like onions (why?), he not only has a very healthy diet but loves and appreciates food in a way even *he* never thought he would. Over the next two days we ate at these restaurants:

Uno Mas: Really good tapas.

Library Street: Just great food in a lovely room.

Fish Shop: Tiny place with about ten seats, including the counter. Amazing oysters. Amazing everything.

Note: Bustling. Delicious.

To have five varied and wonderful meals in a row in almost any city is not easy. But in Dublin it was.

In all the time Aidan and I have spent in each other's company over the years, and with all the traveling we have done individually for work and leisure, we had never ended up together in Ireland, the land of his ancestors, or in Italy, the land of mine. As much as we cherish our ethnic pasts and have spoken about them passionately to each other for decades, we had never taken the time to explore them together. Life must have gotten in the way. But finally, for a couple of days we were here in his homeland, and I got to spend time with my dear talented and generous friend who championed me when we were both young actors and supported me as a person through the toughest times. I got to walk with him and Lizzie, his wife of thirty-five years, through the beautifully lit campus of Trinity College as he told me stories of coming to Dublin and working dreadful jobs to eke out a living as a fledgling thespian and coming to the college to see a play for a couple of quid and eat the bread and soup that came along with the ticket. They were stories that I may well have heard before, during long weekends at his house in upstate New York, where we also rang in many New Year's Eves together around a campfire he would build and lovingly tend to throughout the night, but I didn't care.

May 21

Flew home. Unpacked, did laundry. Hung out with kids. Packed for tomorrow's trip to Italy. I try to avoid back-to-back trips, but I had no choice this time. It's not only the travel itself that's tiring, it's the packing and unpacking that is equally so and, frankly, boring.

May 22

Exercised; went to kids' school assembly, where Millie was given a Golden Book Award for being a great all-around kid, which she is. I headed straight to the airport begrudgingly.

Flew to Milan and then drove an hour and a half to Brescia, where Lottie and some of the crew from *Searching for Italy* had been since the day before.

We were to film some online content for the cookware line that I designed with GreenPan that bears my name, which we've been working on for a while and is coming out in the fall. The company came to me a couple of years ago and asked if I would design a line with them that would be sold basically everywhere, but I wanted something more special that would be sold only in certain shops as well as online, and I insisted that it all had to be made in Italy. Eventually we came to terms, and with their brilliant designer Jan we came up with a design and product that we were all happy with.

I had always wanted to design cookware because I grew up with parents who were as concerned with the aesthetics of their pots and pans as they were with their functionality. (My father even designed and made some of our wooden kitchen utensils.) Luckily, I have inherited a lot of the Scandinavian kitchenware and tableware that they used throughout my childhood.

During the sixties and seventies, Scandi stuff was all the rage. The Danish brand Dansk had a store in Mount Kisco, a nearby town, that we would pop into every now and again. Every other Saturday or so we would run errands as a family, which of course I balked at then but now look back on fondly. These errands might include a stop at the bank, the liquor store, the hardware store, and the Bedford Barn, an eclectic shop that sold everything, including clothing that wasn't tatty at a fair price. We would also stop at Caldor, a now defunct chain of department stores. Caldor was the northeastern US's postwar general store, and I loved wandering its well-stocked aisles, which held everything from clothing to tools, cookware, sports equipment, fishing gear, tents, sneakers, camping stoves, bicycles, bows and their arrows, BB guns, and a wide array of rifles and handguns. A different weapon for everyone in the family. As the old song goes, "that's America to me." At the end of our trip, we would usually stop at the aforementioned Dansk. I can still hear my mother shouting to my father from one end of the house to the other as we readied for our Saturday excursion:

"Stan! Remind me, I want to stop at Dansk because they're having a sale!"

I don't know why she didn't wait until she was in closer proximity to him. Maybe the shouting helped them both remember that she wanted to go there. I wonder if the Danish do the same.

Anyway, Jan the cookware designer, who is not Danish but Dutch, said that he had studied me for months before coming up with the initial designs. What he meant was that he had looked at a lot of the content I had filmed in my kitchen and based his design concept for the line on my cookware, utensils, and furniture, and the color palette in my home. During a couple more meetings, we refined the look and ended up with what I think is a very handsome set of cookware that is nonstick and PFA-free. You're welcome.

The folks at Williams Sonoma, who were going to sell the line exclusively, took us to a lovely dinner in Brescia, a city that seemed to be not only very wealthy but also maybe the cleanest I'd ever seen on the Italian peninsula.

The food was very good, but there was so much of it that my stomach shut down after the third course and I could not eat the beautiful *tagliata* that the chef brought out. But I had been well sated with the sweetest prosciutto, pasta, risotto, and white wine.

May 23

We filmed in the Lumenflon factory itself, which turns out over eight million pieces of cookware a year for different companies.

May 24

Today we went to a home we had rented where I was to put the cookware into action by making different dishes using as many of the pots and pans as possible. All of it would be filmed. We chose recipes from our cookbooks so we could shamelessly sell more of those as well. This is what I made:

Fresh tomato sauce with spaghetti

Asparagus risotto

Chicken cacciatore

Steak oreganato

Fish stew

The cookware performed even better than I could have hoped for. And somehow all the food tasted good, which doesn't always happen when you are cooking just to capture content and imagery. After nine hours of nonstop cooking (my favorite activity) and posing for photos (my least favorite activity), I was tired but very relieved that the cookware worked so well.

This evening we ate in a restaurant that was terrible.

Actually, *fucking* terrible.

It was so bad that I can't even remember what I didn't eat.

The chef (and I use the term loosely) was obviously trying to put a "spin" on some local classics. All I can say is that things had spun out of control, because he had clearly lost all sense of what good food is supposed to be. Besides that, everything was served on oversize, slightly concave rectangular plates, which is a sure sign that the food will be awful. If you see those in any restaurant, do not cross that threshold.

Why people feel the need to reinvent the wheel when they know nothing about physics is beyond me. In this case that goes for the plates *and* the food.

A simple plate.

A simple bowl.

A simple fork.

A simple spoon.

A simple knife.

Then just make good food. Simply.

That's all one should want and all one needs.

If anyone wants or needs more than that, they should reassess their values.

It's that simple.

May 25

I flew back home feeling quite tired. I do find traveling enervating, but as I've said, packing for a trip is possibly even worse, especially nowadays. The decanting of liquids and creams into the appropriate-size containers if one is traveling with only carry-on luggage takes far too long. But inevitably, no matter how thorough one has been, there is one tube or bottle or sharp object that one has forgotten at the bottom of a bag that gets discovered by the scanner, and the embarrassing process of a blue-gloved security officer rifling through one's intimate garments begins. Although some airports now have new machines that are somehow able to discern a nefarious liquid, gel, or cream from its benign lookalikes, making the whole process much quicker and more civilized, not enough terminals have those. So, the searches continue. In the evening we went to Scott's in Richmond with some friends. There's also a Scott's in Mayfair that is wonderful, and this one lived up to the other's reputation.

May 26

Packed up the car for a week in the Cotswolds with the kids. We always pack pasta, canned tomato, beans, a five-liter can of our favorite olive oil, the largest saucepan I have, risotto rice, wine, booze, a set of kitchen tongs, and my favorite knife. (I stupidly forgot to pack Parmigiano and kosher salt.) We do this because those foodstuffs are our staples, and we bring the kitchenware because most houses, no matter how grand they are or how much you pay for them, have kitchens that are usually poorly outfitted, and inevitably we end up buying pans, colanders, etc., so now we just pack our own. It's a strange thing about many British houses: all the money goes into the edifice and the garden, but the kitchen is an afterthought. I was pleased to see when we arrived at this house that this was not the case.

We're here with our friends Anita and Heinrich, who have three lovely children, ages fifteen, eleven, and five. If they weren't lovely, we would not holiday with them. If people don't have a like style of parenting to ours, I have difficulty spending more than a single night together. By that I mean having very basic rules for your kids. Proper meals, mealtimes, bedtimes, and polite behavior, saying please and thank you, etc. That's it. I know parenting is never easy and every kid is different, but children need and want structure, and it is our obligation to give it to them. I am hardly perfect as a parent, but I always try my best to be fun, fair, and firm, and sometimes I'm successful. Maybe I'm being too idealistic or old-fashioned, but I hate bratty kids and lazy parents.

Anyway, our friends' kids are great as usual, so I don't know what I'm going on about.

I expect the week will be filled with cooking. Anita graduated from Leiths the year prior after dabbling in indifferent professions and taking time off to raise the kids. Her parents are from eastern India, but she grew up in Texas, and she is a wonderful cook, now a bona fide chef and a food obsessive.

They arrived a few hours after we did and were very hungry, so I made a ton of pasta marinara.

May 27

This morning Anita made a frittata, which she burned because she had put milk in it (not necessary at all and I should have said something) and didn't move it continuously. We salvaged it by cutting off the unintended char and it was pretty good.

Soon after breakfast, Anita and I went to a farmers' market and bought spareribs, pork tenderloins, a whole chicken, and lots of vegetables. She marinated all the pork in ginger, olive oil, garlic, and some other stuff that I wasn't privy to and put it in the fridge to sit for two days. I roasted the chicken so we could make chicken salad and use the carcass to make stock for risotto or whatever.

At night I made pasta with zucchini because everyone loves it after seeing it made on *Searching for Italy*. Frying the zucchini in batches is time-consuming but well worth it in the end.

May 28

For breakfast: eggs poached in marinara with a side of asparagus. Delicious.

Felicity, organized as ever, reserved a table at a nearby pub for a classic Sunday roast. It was a lovely, rather upscale, cozy place that had received several accolades over the years for its food and drink. We ordered and were all very excited, but then things took a bit of a turn. Our food was delayed for an inordinate amount of time because a customer had spilled a beer over the computer system or something, a fact that we only found out about upon our departure.

Luckily the kids' food had come straightaway, their order having been put in pre-spill, I guess. As we waited and waited and waited, we did find it strange that no staff member ever alerted us that there would be a delay or explained what had happened. We kept asking our servers for the food, only to be told that they would check on it. But I guess they never *really* checked, because they would disappear yet again for another fifteen minutes. After we'd been waiting for an hour and a half, the food finally came. I had hake with samphire, which probably took all of seven minutes to cook. It was just okay. Other people had other things, like meat, but I was too irritated to care. The chips were good.

In the end the owner's apologies were tepid at best and he didn't do what any good restaurateur would do, which is not charge for the wine or the dessert or something by way of compensating us for the long wait. In Italy they would *overcompensate*. (Although in Italy the whole thing would never have happened in the first place, let's face it.) And this was a proper award-winning gastropub. We were miffed and out almost £400. I don't think we'll be going back. Also, with that many people it's not worth going out that often. Good restaurants are few and far between in the countryside, which can mean a long drive on winding roads, which with children is not always pleasant, especially when one is prone to carsickness like Millie. So, on holidays like this we usually end up staying in and cooking, which suits me just fine.

May 29–June 2

Here are some of the things we cooked throughout the rest of the week:

Zucchini fritters

Tomato salad

Gnocchi (homemade by Felicity) with pesto and green beans

Barbecued ribs and marinated pork tenderloins

Risotto with asparagus and zucchini

Burgers

Vegetable soup, using the chicken stock we made

Anita and I made the soup together. Here's what we used and how we did it:

Tucci Minestrone

Extra-virgin olive oil
1 large yellow onion, diced
1 large red onion, chopped
2 cloves garlic, chopped
3 celery stalks, diced
3 small leeks, chopped
3 small spring onions, chopped
3 carrots, diced
2 medium zucchini, diced
2 quarts chicken stock or vegetable stock
6 pomodorini, quartered
2 large potatoes, cut into small cubes
2 bunches spring greens (chard or cavolo nero can be substituted)
4 basil leaves
1 Parmigiano-Reggiano rind (about the size of your palm)
Salt
Freshly ground black pepper
2 (14-ounce) cans or jars precooked cannellini beans (optional)
2 cups fresh or frozen peas (defrosted)
2 to 3 cups grated Parmigiano-Reggiano or Pecorino
1 cup chopped parsley

- Pour some olive oil in a large pot. Add the onions, garlic, celery, leeks, and spring onions and sauté over medium-low heat until they have softened. Add the carrots and zucchini and cook for another 5 minutes.

- Add the stock and bring it to a boil. Add the tomatoes, potatoes, greens, basil, Parmigiano rind, and salt and pepper to taste. Reduce the heat to a low boil and cook for 20 to 30 minutes, stirring occasionally. (The beans can be added at this time if you're using them.) After 15 minutes, add the peas and cook for another 5 to 10 minutes.

- Serve in large bowls with croutons, the grated Parmigiano or Pecorino, a drizzle of EVOO, and a sprinkle of the chopped parsley.

Hearty.
Healthy.

June 1

On our last night, Felicity invited some folks from the production of *Rivals*, including the lovely David Tennant, whom we had gotten to know when we did *Inside Man* together a couple of years ago. We made grilled eggplant and five large T-bone steaks seared on the griddle because the barbecue was too far away and we were behind schedule (and it was not a regular barbecue but a Big Green Egg, which I still haven't learned how to use even though I've owned one for eight years), along with roasted potatoes with garlic, olive oil, and rosemary.

At one point Matteo came to the table and I suddenly remembered that David had narrated all the *How to Train Your Dragon* books by Cressida Cowell, which Matteo has listened to for years. When I told Matteo a while ago that I knew David, he'd just looked at me with great suspicion, but here was David, that brilliant, lanky, seemingly ageless Scotsman, in the flesh, to prove I wasn't just bandying his name about erroneously. It took Matteo a minute to grasp that the voice he had heard for so long and so often was generated by a thing of flesh and blood called an actor who sat next to him. When it finally clicked, his eyes widened, and he just stared. He then asked David to do the voice of Toothless, one of the dragons in the series. David sweetly obliged and Matteo's eyes grew even wider. I think my son slept very well that night. Or maybe not at all. David probably had nightmares about dragons and Vikings who all sounded very much like him.

June 5

Had a Zoom meeting with Francesco Mazzei and Ambassador Lambertini to continue discussing the royal feast for my soon-to-be new best friend King Charles that we'll be throwing at some point. I said that I thought our original idea of alternating British and Italian dishes seemed a bit contrived and would be a recipe for overfeeding. Instead, I suggested that we create a proper Italian menu using as many British ingredients as possible, which is something Francesco has tried to do over the last few years in his restaurants. Here are some of the dishes I suggested (obviously the choices would be dictated by the season in which the event takes place):

Risotto con funghi: Autumn

Gnocchi with samphire: Spring/summer

Tagliata (grilled beef steak): Year-round

Salt-encrusted sea bass: Year-round

Cod or haddock livornese: Year-round

Pasta con vongole: Month-dependent

Frittata: Year-round

Roast lamb: Best in spring

Fruit tart: Spring, summer, autumn

Baked ham (gammon) with mostarda di frutta: Year-round

Certain ingredients will obviously need to come from Italy, like olive oil, Parmigiano, rice for risotto (arborio, carnaroli, or vialone nano), and probably tomatoes, but we could basically find all the other ingredients we needed right here in the British Isles to make these classic Italian dishes. For instance, the sea bass can come from the southern and western waters of the UK; delicious eggs from the Crown's own duchy; the lamb from Wales; the pork from anywhere in England; the beef from Scotland or Herefordshire. The herbs—rosemary, thyme, parsley—are easily found here, and Maldon sea salt from Essex is one of the best salts in the world. (Okay, ideally you would want to a use an Amalfi lemon instead of one grown in a British walled garden or greenhouse, but one must be flexible.)

It was decided that Francesco would peruse these options and put them into a cohesive menu. The ambassador would then send out an invitation explaining the intention of the night, which is basically a celebration of British produce and Italian cookery in honor of HRH King Charles. If the dinner indeed happens, I will tell all.*

* The king canceled dinner. That's okay. There are many monarchs in the sea.

June 7

Meeting at the Groucho Club with Executive Chef Erion. We spoke via Zoom a while ago about me curating a menu with Erion for eighty or so members, before which I would be interviewed. The Groucho, now under new ownership, has been doing these events with different chefs over the last year or so.

The Groucho Club is aptly named for the king of comedy, Groucho Marx, who once said, "I don't want to belong to any club that will accept me as a member." Opened by a group of friends in the literary world as an alternative to the stuffy, posh, men-only clubs in 1985, it is still going strong. I was first taken there in 2000 by the cast of an HBO film that I was filming called *Conspiracy* by my cast members, including Kenneth Branagh, Kevin McNally, and my now longtime friend and sometime on-screen lover, Colin Firth, and a great time was had by all.

At the Groucho meeting I was told that I was to be interviewed by the witty author, presenter, and food critic Grace Dent, whom I've always wanted to meet. I reviewed the menu we had discussed a while ago and looked at the kitchen and the dining rooms where everything would take place. As the event will be in August, we decided the menu that follows would be appropriate:

Carciofi alla romana

Focaccia

Honeydew melon with prosciutto

Spaghetti alle vongole

Cod alla livornese

Prosecco granita

Fresh fruit

Just as a note: *Carciofi* (artichokes) *alla romana* differ from those *alla giudia* that I described earlier. This recipe is usually made with small purple artichokes. They are first stripped of their outermost leaves, the stems trimmed so that just an inch or so remains, the inner beard scooped out, and the cavity stuffed with just a bit of chopped mint, garlic, salt, and pepper. They are then boiled until they are very soft and dressed with olive oil. Then you eat them. Then they melt in your mouth. Then you are really happy.

June 8

Lottie and I had a meeting with the general manager of a hotel who is interested in having me open a restaurant there. I have always wanted to open a restaurant but ideally something small. Felicity hates the idea no matter what the size because it is an enormous amount of work and almost always a lose/lose venture. This is a large space, but with the hotel footing the bill for renovations and so on, it's a hard thing not to consider. I have an idea for a chef who might be the perfect fit, who was actually Lottie's idea for a chef who might be the perfect fit. It would of course be an Italian restaurant. A slightly upscale trattoria serving seasonal dishes from all of Italy's regions. Not fussy, not fancy. Just good. If it happens before I finish this book, I will reveal more.*

After the meeting, Lottie and I had lunch at a dumpling place we had eaten in a while back. It was good but not quite as good as we remembered. Although the shrimp fried rice was excellent. I could eat shrimp fried rice every day. I have made it several times with some success but not consistently. I am slightly intimidated by making dishes that aren't Italian or at least Mediterranean. I don't know why. Maybe because I'd have to expand the ingredients in my larder or maybe because I'm often too distracted to follow a recipe. But I think that because I understand Italian food, if I follow a recipe and it seems like something is missing or it doesn't taste quite right, I'll know how to rectify it. With

* I declined the offer to open a restaurant. Too much work for not enough return.

other cuisines I wouldn't have a clue. So out of fear, I cling to what I know. My acting teacher always encouraged us to "go beyond what's comfortable," not just as actors but as people. I have made a conscious choice to follow his advice in my work and in other aspects of my life over the years, but not so much in the kitchen. I guess it's time I started. It means I am going to have to plan meals ahead of time. God help me.

In the afternoon we discovered wild garlic growing in the garden. (It's just our small backyard but the British call it a garden, which sounds better.) We planted some a year ago and thought it had all died, but apparently some of it lived. Our gardener pointed it out; it was half-hidden by some shrubs. He cut off all the leaves, put them in the sink to soak, then transplanted a few of the plants to an even shadier spot by Felicity's office where we hoped they would flourish.

I adore wild garlic. Its flowers are bright white and delicate, and its aroma powerful and somewhat intoxicating. I first came across it when I was making a terrible film in the English countryside. One day as I made my way back to base camp through the ancient wood where we were filming, I saw a carpet of white flowers and fine, spear-shaped green leaves on either side of the footpath. Before I could comment on their beauty I was confronted with a potent smell. The person I was with told me it was a patch of wild garlic. I was entranced. I had no idea there even was such a plant. Its closest relative would be ramps, which I also love, and although their taste is suggestive of garlic, ramps are related to leeks and onions. Soon afterward I tasted wild garlic and have sought it out ever since in woodlands and markets whenever it's in season.

With this unexpected, albeit small, very welcome bounty from our garden, I decided to make pesto by hand, and not in the blender. Once Matteo saw what I was doing he asked to join in. I think he just wanted to get his hot little hands on the mezzaluna I was using. I hesitated at first, but after impressing upon him how sharp the implement was, I showed him how to use it. It's not an easy task for anyone, let alone an eight-year-old, to carry out, but he did well, although he did a lot more "chopping" with it than "rocking." While he was engrossed, I chopped up a handful of parsley, a handful of basil, and some Parmigiano. We then threw the results of our efforts into a marble mortar and pestle, and I demonstrated to him how to grind it all together.

Chopping something with a sharp blade and smashing something with a dense stone are very satisfying activities for a growing boy. Why didn't I think of harnessing this young man's burgeoning aggression in this way before? As Matteo worked his inchoate testosterone into the marble, I slowly drizzled extra-virgin olive oil into the mixture. The result was a verdant paste of tangy earthiness or earthy tanginess.

As it was nearing the kids' dinnertime, I boiled some pasta and tossed it with the pesto, and Matteo ate a bowl and a half of it. A satisfying experience for both father and son.

Millie refused to touch it and had pasta with butter and cheese. Maybe next year.

June 10

Alone with Millie and Matteo as Felicity is on a sort of retreat in Bordeaux with two colleagues, something I almost believed was true.

I made crepes that morning for them, some slathered with Nutella, others sprinkled with sugar and a squeeze of lemon. The first one came out well but the following few were embarrassing failures about which the kids were kindly sympathetic. (Felicity usually makes them and I make American pancakes.) Only after I discarded the copper pan especially designed for making them and switched to a small stainless-steel one did I have success. I ate one and it was good. The kids were happy, and my embarrassment disappeared until the next time I would commit another culinary faux pas.

As it was going to be a hot weekend, I filled up a new paddling pool for the kids, then took them to a local pizza place for lunch. The owner hails from Naples and makes an excellent classic *pizza napoletana*. They ordered focaccia as Millie hates tomato sauce (who is this person?) and Matteo seems to prefer only Pizza Express and the like. They ate just about everything, including a large plate of prosciutto. I had a pizza with tomato sauce, basil, and ricotta, which was delicious. After the meal, as they each clutched a cup of mango sorbet in their oily little hands, we walked home.

* * *

In the evening, Lottie and her friends, the wonderful actress Sophie McShera and her beau Otis, were coming for an early dinner. I wasn't quite sure what I was going to make. I wanted to throw a steak I had in the fridge on the barbecue, but it was so bloody hot out that I couldn't bear the thought of it, and besides, Sophie is a pescatarian, so I nixed that idea. Then I noticed a bunch of Tropea onions in the basket of related alliums. How they got there I don't know, but I was thrilled.

Tropea onions come from the west coast of Calabria and can only be grown in a small area (the environs of the town of Tropea) that has a singular kind of sandy soil. Shaped like a shallot with a skin that is a deep reddish purple, they are so sweet that they can be plucked out of the ground, peeled, and eaten like an apple. I did so myself when we filmed a segment about them, and the taste was extraordinary. I figured since they were sitting right in front of me today, I'd make a vegetarian recipe that I learned while filming the same segment.

After calling the fishmonger and asking them to hold two small sea bass for me that I would make as our main course, I got to work setting the table while the kids ate frozen-fruit ice pops standing naked in the paddling pool. This was the meal I ended up making:

Spaghetti with Tropea Onion

- I thinly sliced the onions and sautéed them in EVOO with a clove of thinly sliced garlic. As they cooked down, I periodically added a bit of vegetable broth that I had just made with carrot, celery, onion, and salt about 20 minutes before. I then combined it in a large saucepan with cooked spaghetti and tossed it with Parmigiano, Romano, and chopped basil.

Roasted/Baked Sea Bass

- I stuffed the scaled and gutted sea bass (heads and tails still on) with slices of lemon, salt, rosemary, thyme, parsley, and garlic and coated them with EVOO inside and out, then scattered about 10 pomodorini around them. I baked them for a bit, then put them under the broiler for a few minutes.

Salad

- Cucumber, celery, and thinly sliced fennel with a lemon vinaigrette.

Somehow it all timed out well (timing a meal not usually being my strong point, especially when I am cooking alone) and it was delicious. Lottie said it was the best sea bass I had ever made. *Why not believe her?* I thought.

June 11

For breakfast, I baked frozen croissants for the kids, which I find are often better than most of the fresh ones you get in overpriced cafés in London. As it's Sunday, I cleared out the vegetable drawer so it could be replenished the next day.

I roasted the remaining small potatoes and carrots with garlic and onions, rosemary, thyme, and EVOO. I utilized the waning leeks, spring onions, and larger potatoes by making a potato-leek soup (as it can be eaten hot or, my preference, chilled) and sautéed the last few red peppers with some onions and a splash of rosé that I had been nipping at, along with a couple of sautéed chicken breasts. I thought this would give Felicity some light but hearty dishes to choose from when she returned from her Gallic roistering.

Upon her arrival, she was delighted to see the children of course, smothered them with hugs and kisses, cursorily pecked me on the cheek, and started to eat. Soon afterward, as we all watched a Harry Potter film, she promptly fell asleep beside a wide-awake Millie.

Seems that someone had a busy weekend. I chose to remain in ignorant bliss.

June 12

I met the curators of the National Portrait Gallery, who were kind enough to give me a private tour of the upcoming Paul McCartney photography exhibition, *Eyes of the Storm*. I'm to interview him before an audience of students to promote the exhibition as well as the newly renovated space. I met the former Beatle over twenty-two years ago at Aidan Quinn's house. Through coincidence, his daughter Mary has become a dear friend. The exhibit at the National Portrait Gallery was wonderful. It consisted of images taken by a brilliant young man experimenting with photography as he documented moments that would change not only music but the world forever.

After leaving the National Portrait Gallery I was famished, having eaten little for breakfast. I didn't want to go to a restaurant for lunch as I wanted to get home to write about what I am writing about right now, but I needed to eat something, and I didn't just want to grab a shitty sandwich, so I did what I didn't want to do and went to a restaurant for lunch. I headed directly for J. Sheekey, a West End institution that has been around since 1896.

Pass beneath the memorable red awnings that carry its name and you will find an elegant, intimate restaurant and oyster bar of old with leather banquettes, white tablecloths, and walls covered in black-and-white photos of famous actors and actresses of the British stage. Although not inexpensive, it is a welcome respite from the many chain restaurants that line the streets and alleys of the theater district. The menu is fish-forward.

I ordered a Scottish lager, which was rich and quite potent, along with two appetizers, pea soup and tempura prawns. I was so tempted to order the fish and chips because I know it's excellent. However, it's also a sizable portion and I knew if I ate it, I would be fighting off sleep for most of the afternoon, and I needed to do a few things, like write this book and other stuff that unemployed actors do.

I drank the lager and ate the soup and the prawns, all of which were excellent. The soup needed a bit of salt, so I added a little, but I find that sometimes when one adds salt to soup after it's cooked, one ends up tasting only the salt. Is that just me? Anyway, it was the right amount of food to fill me up but not drag me down.

June 13

Felicity, Lottie, Isabel, Nicolo, some friends, and I all went to see Harry Styles at Wembley.

Staggering.

It's as though he has the combined talent, charm, and energy of every great musician and performer who has ever made music or performed.

And he's a nice person.

And he loves Italian food.

And he loves to cook.

And he's our friend.

And we love him.

Who the f— doesn't?

June 16

Lottie and I left for a trip to Aspen, Colorado. After checking in at the airport, we were given an option of lounges, and I chose the Cathay Pacific lounge. Having flown that airline many times years ago from NYC to Vancouver while making a film of questionable quality, I knew that the food was always better than most.

In the lounge, Lottie and I both had the "Chinese Set," which consisted of two different steamed dumplings and a steamed bun with a mincemeat-like filling, a vegetable noodle stir-fry, and a bowl of chicken-and-mushroom congee.

I love congee. I first had it over thirty-five years ago in Vancouver working on a TV show. Vancouver has a huge Chinese population, more than ever now since the British lease of Hong Kong expired, and the Asian produce and food there is extraordinary. Congee was a part of the breakfasts on set, and I couldn't get enough of it.

For those unacquainted, congee is rice that is cooked slowly, for a long time in a large amount of water, so it basically takes on a porridge-like consistency. Because it is even more bland than porridge, its flavor must be augmented with mushrooms, seafood, vegetables, spring onions, and so on. It is a comfort food that is supposedly very good for you, and if that is true, then that is wonderful. If not, I am not so sure I care. I'll eat it anyway.

Ten hours to Dallas. Two-hour layover. One and a half hours to Aspen. Both flights delayed. Total of twenty-one hours of travel. Shoot me.

* * *

Finally, we arrived in Aspen. The last time I was here was over a decade ago for the Aspen Ideas Festival. Along with Wren Arthur (whom I'd met through Robert Altman) and Steve Buscemi, with whom I had a production company at the time, I organized a panel of doctors and scientists from around the world to discuss standard-of-care and alternative cancer treatments. We were in the early stages of making a documentary about the subject, which sadly we were unable to bring to fruition. On the panel were my dear friend Niven Narain, a scientist who is the head of a company that is making huge strides in non-toxic treatments for cancer and other diseases, and Dr. Shimon Slavin from Hadassah Hospital in Jerusalem, who had treated Kate a few years before with a protocol not available in the States.

Although Dr. Slavin's efforts were obviously not successful, I have never been so impressed with one doctor's determination, honesty, and kindness in treating a patient whose chances of survival were minimal at best. What a truly extraordinary man.

In the few days before Kate began the brutal treatment regimen, we were able to explore Jerusalem a bit. We had been told by someone that there was a Palestinian hummus place in the Old City that we needed to try. So, we did.

It was a tiny restaurant with about ten small tables, which I think served only hummus, pita bread, and cucumber-tomato salads. The décor consisted of plastic-wrapped pallets of bottled water and soft drinks. To the right of the entrance was a small counter, on top of which sat an enormous copper vat of hummus, its rim and upper inside walls encrusted with the vestiges of hummuses gone by. Instantly I feared that a bout of food poisoning was postprandially assured. I could not have been more wrong. Not only was all well afterward, but it was delicious.

Hummus is everywhere these days, from posh restaurants to fast-food joints, and like so many of us, I have eaten my fair share of it. However, I now know that unless I return to that spot and sup from that ancient pot, I will never have hummus as good as that ever again.

Being in Aspen brought back many fond memories. I was given an award at the film festival about a dozen years ago, and Kate and I skied there. The skiing was amazing, as well as the food, particularly at Nobu and a little French restaurant on the slopes where, had everyone not been speaking English and wearing ten-gallon hats, one would have sworn one was in Verbier. (I've never been.) Raclette and *vin blanc* were very much on hand and in mouths.

After the arduous trip, Lottie and I finally arrived at the hotel. Having not eaten for too long, I rang room service and ordered chicken soup and a hamburger. By the time I cleaned myself up and unpacked, the food had arrived, and I wolfed it down. A terrible thing to do right before bed, but sometimes a necessary one. You can wake up in the middle of the night either because you're hungry or because you've eaten too much. I prefer the latter. I suppose I could have ordered a Caesar salad as a happy medium. Next trip. But I doubt it.

June 17

Having awakened early, I went to the gym and had a breakfast even higher in cholesterol than my dinner. Poached eggs, very buttery hash browns, toast, and avocado.

Shot some photos and short videos for San Pellegrino at the Food and Wine fest and then had lunch at a seafood restaurant, which was good. Tasted three different kinds of oysters, but sadly two of them, from Prince Edward Island, tasted metallic and flat. The Ichiban from Washington State were great, but none matched the mollusks of Bordeaux. Where's the French coast when you need it?

June 18

Flying home made the first leg of the trip seem like a picnic. It went like this:

Flight to Dallas from Aspen canceled due to mechanical issues and lack of mechanics to deal with those issues.

Got new flight just in time to Chicago O'Hare, where we would no longer transfer to an American Airlines flight to London but would instead transfer to a British Airways flight to London.

Told we also have seats reserved on a later American Airlines flight if we miss connection.

Landed at Chicago O'Hare Terminal 1 with about forty minutes to make connecting flight in Terminal 5.

Chicago O'Hare airport covers over seventy-five hundred acres.

Caught train to Terminal 5.

Went through security.

Ran to gate 17 in Terminal 5.

Gate 17 advertises a flight to Stockholm, not London.

We are told the BA London flight is leaving from gate 33.

Run to gate 33.

Chicago O'Hare airport covers over seventy-five hundred acres.

Lots of people shout out my name as I hurtle by.

I'm embarrassed.

Air-conditioning not working from gate 17 onward.

Arrive at gate 33 soaked with our own sweat and probably other people's as well.

Gate opens for boarding.

We present our boarding cards.

Told to go to the desk at the gate as our passports need to be rechecked.

Self-consciously leave the queue under the gaze of many.

Step up to the desk and hand over our passports.

Charming gatekeeper winces and shakes her head often as she types info into the computer.

Tells us she cannot find us in the system.

We explain that someone changed our flight for us from American Airlines to British Airways.

She says she needs to call a supervisor.

The supervisor arrives.

He shakes his head even more than the gatekeeper did, but he is charmless.

Very.

He tells us our seats have been given away, but he doesn't know how or why or when.

Says he cannot help us at all.

Says that American Airlines gave away our seats and probably put us on the later flight because they assumed we would miss our connection.

Charmlessly, he says we must go to the American Airlines desk.

We realize in that moment that he is not just charmless.

He's a dick.

We ask where the American Airlines desk is.

Terminal 3, he says.

I can sense glee beneath his lack of affect.

Actually, he's a *real* dick.

We leave the desk for Terminal 3.

Chicago O'Hare covers over seventy-five hundred acres.

We walk stoically toward our destination.

Lots of people shout out my name as I pass by.

This makes me uncomfortable.

We arrive at the end of Terminal 5.

We ask a cheery security guard how to get to Terminal 3.

He tells us we can avoid going through security again if we head the way he is pointing and present our boarding passes to the guard there.

We tell him we don't have boarding passes.

He looks at us sadly.

He says we have no choice but to go the long way round and that we will have to go through security again.

We thank him.

He tells us that he is sorry and that he hopes our day gets better.

He is not a dick.

He is nice.

The other guy is still a dick.

We walk the long way round.

Take the tram to Terminal 3.

Go to the American Airlines desk and check in.

Nice young fellow confirms that there are indeed tickets for us on the later flight.

But only *I* am in business class.

Lottie has been relegated to premium economy.

We ask for an upgrade.

We are told business class is full.

Lottie is despondent.

She is not fussy about such things usually, but it is a long-haul overnight flight, and I don't blame her.

The ability to be supine for over eight hours on a plane makes a huge difference, let's face it.

We go through security.

Go to the lounge.

The nice man at the desk tells Lottie he will keep her updated as to an upgrade.

The lounge has the warmth of a midlevel corporation's boardroom.

I look for the bar.

I see the buffet.

Jesus Christ.

No.

I know I will never erase its image from my mind.

I find the self-serve bar and pour a scotch.

Averting my eyes from the horror of the buffet, I grab a very white roll from the bread basket to coat my stomach.

Lottie eats a banana and three cubes of cheese.

I worry she might become constipated.

She says she doesn't care.

We wait.

Sip bottled water and scotch and gnaw on the roll.

A supervisor finds us and apologizes for the all the trouble.

She is lovely and nice.

Not like that other supervisor, who was a dick.

She tells Lottie that they should be able to give her an upgrade at the gate.

We are happier.

She says she will give us a buggy ride to the gate.

We get a buggy ride to the gate.

The buggy has a long pole with a yellow flashing light and emits an extremely loud beeping sound.

This calls a tremendous amount of attention to the buggy.

Even more people shout my name.

Now *I* feel like a dick.

We get to the gate.

The gatekeeper says Lottie must sit in her premium economy seat and then move to business.

Don't know why.

Don't really care.

As I enter the gateway a gatekeeper asks if I am seated in 6D.

I check my sweaty boarding pass.

I am.

He tells me that my TV monitor is not working.

My heart almost sinks but it doesn't have the energy.

Lottie says she will switch seats with me as she won't watch anything anyway.

We board.

Lottie gets the upgrade.

We switch seats.

I start a crossword puzzle.

The lights in the cabin go dark.

We are told that there is an electrical power issue and that it should only take a few minutes to repair.

The cabin begins to heat up due to lack of air-conditioning.

We wait on the tarmac for two hours.

They remedy the problem.

We still don't move.

The head flight attendant gets on the intercom and tells us that there is no drinking water on the plane, and we can't take off without drinking water.

She's not wrong.

Although at this point, I'm willing to risk it.

I overhear her call someone in the terminal in a fit of pique and tell them that her pleas for drinking water have gone unanswered by three different departments.

The water arrives moments later.

The flight attendants take their positions and prepare for departure.

I take a sleeping pill and prepare to watch *John Wick: Chapter 4.*

June 22

Felicity and I drove four hours to the south of England, where we recently purchased a house. It's a "fixer-upper" to put it mildly. It will take at least two and a half years and most of our income to make it livable. I may well be in a care home by then. If I can afford a care home. What was I thinking?

We are to visit the house with the architect and engineer early tomorrow morning, so we drove down this evening and are staying in a little hotel called Highcliffe House run by a wonderful couple. After checking in we ate in a place called the Old Bank.

The tiny restaurant is run by Liam, a twenty-two-year-old fellow who opened it a couple of years before while the pandemic was still rearing its ugly head. He and his father, who is a builder, renovated it themselves. It is primarily a steak restaurant, with all the meat and just about everything else sourced locally.

This is what we ate:

Starters: Oxtail arancini, salt-and-pepper calamari

My main: Braised pieces of pork belly and tenderloin

Felicity's main: Rib eye steak with béarnaise

All of it was lovely. Did I mention that Liam is only twenty-two? I have socks older than he is. The fact that this young man has been able to create and sustain an excellent eight-table restaurant in a sleepy, rather-hard-to-reach town on the heels of a pandemic is an astonishing achievement. We were both very impressed. When I was that age, I was wandering around Manhattan hoping someone might give me the opportunity to practice the noble vocation for which I had trained so hard, pretending to be someone else. Tragic when you think about it, even without the comparison.

June 23

We spent the day at the house with the architect, the engineer, the landscapers. I am very excited about the prospect of creating a home where we can spend time together as a family, where friends and extended family can come for long weekends, where I can build an art studio and an auxiliary kitchen in which to film a cooking show that has been percolating in my hungry mind for a while now, where we can plant a vegetable garden and a small orchard and put the benefits of them to good use every season, where my daughters, or sons, can get married, where Felicity can bring her lover(s), where my proctologist(s) can visit, and where our grandchildren can spend time with their cousins for years to come when I am no longer here. Realizing all the above will take quite a while and a fair amount of the "great bourgeois long green"; I hope the fickle finger of Hollywood doesn't turn against me for at least another decade.

June 24

Driving home, we stopped at a motorway service area and ordered two sausage rolls and a Cornish pasty from a van there. They were not half bad. Then we hit traffic, which was more than half bad, and a four-hour trip turned into a five-and-a-half-hour slog.

June 25

The kids watched television while we did a painful but necessary yoga session with Monique. Got the kids dressed and went to our local farmers' market. Ate a tortilla and some gazpacho that we bought from a Spanish fellow who has been at the market for many years. Both delicious. Bought lots of chicken breasts, a steak, and bags of baby zucchini. We were to cook all of it that day for our friends Blake Lively and Ryan Reynolds, who have recently arrived and are staying about a mile and a half from us in a house that Felicity found for them. Their whole family is here, including their new addition. Blake is delirious from lack of sleep and Ryan is exhausted from filming the third Deadpool movie. We thought it would be nice for them to have a home-cooked meal in their rented house. Our kids didn't really know each other but they all got along well, which makes everyone's life a hell of a lot easier, let's face it.

In their ill-equipped kitchen (another expensive, sprawling English manse for rent with a paltry supply of cookware), we somehow made *spaghetti con zucchine alla Nerano* and then cooked the chicken breasts as follows:

Chicken Cutlets

SERVES 4

4 large chicken breasts
Salt
2 or 3 eggs (enough to coat the chicken)
2 to 4 cups plain breadcrumbs
Olive oil (not extra-virgin)
Lemon wedges, for serving

- Remove the "finger" from each chicken breast. Slice the chicken breasts lengthwise. Place them, 2 at a time, between two pieces of parchment paper and pound them gently so that they are about half of their original thickness. (You can make them thinner if that is your preference.) Do the same with the rest, as well as the "fingers."
- Salt the chicken pieces and set them aside.
- Whisk the eggs in a small bowl.
- Put the breadcrumbs on a large plate.
- Dip each piece of chicken into the egg and then into the breadcrumbs. Set aside on a plate.
- When all the chicken has been breaded, heat up a large flat-bottomed pan over medium-low heat and pour in about ½ cup of the oil. When the oil is hot, add a few pieces of the chicken and cook on both sides until golden brown (leave space in between the pieces; otherwise they will not cook properly). Place the cooked

chicken pieces on a platter. You will have to work in batches and continue to add oil as necessary. When all the chicken has cooked, serve immediately with lemon wedges and a green salad.

Note: You can also use panko breadcrumbs or a mixture or both panko and plain.

These cutlets are also perfect for a picnic lunch as sandwiches in a baguette or good Italian bread. Butter, mustard or mayonnaise, sliced tomato, and lettuce are great with them.

Blake also poached some thin asparagus in butter. A squeeze of lemon over both heightened all the flavors. The kids ate chicken and pasta with butter and cheese. We fried up the steak for Ryan, who's on a high-protein diet. (God, he bores me.) Basically, we all ate a lot. Blake loves to eat and must do so more than ever as a small person is feeding off her day and night.

By the time we finished, it was evening, so we piled the kids into the car, hoping Millie would not throw up on the way home as she often does even on short trips. To be safe we handed her the plastic bag that we keep handy for such occasions and set off. We arrived home without a digestive disaster.

As I read through my entries, I realize that I keep mentioning Millie's penchant for pasta with butter and cheese because she eats it so often. I can't blame her. This simple triumvirate is eaten by kids and adults every day all around the world. I'm not talking about macaroni and cheese and its many iterations, which is an altogether different thing; I'm referring to pasta (almost any shape) with butter and Parmigiano cheese. It has pleased picky eaters and comforted the ailing and the anxious for as long as those three ingredients have been around, which is probably pretty f—ing long. Why? Perhaps because it's so simple it helps us focus on what is necessary: comfort and health. Eating a simple dish gives one clarity. Pasta with butter and cheese laughs in the face of our complex lives.

June 26

Felicity is in NYC for a week. I know she has work to do and is doing it more brilliantly than ever, but I hate her not being around. Huge parts of life are empty without her. I love being with the kids alone, but I love it more when we are all together. She makes everything better.

June 27

Cooked the usual stuff for the kids this week. One night, Matteo requested *spaghetti con tonno* (tuna), which I was more than happy to make for him. Millie was brought to the brink of tears when she heard this was to be her evening meal, but when I told her she only need have a small bowl of it, after which she could then have a bowl of pasta with butter and cheese, the flow of tears was stemmed.

Spaghetti con tonno has been one of my favorite meals since I was a kid. This is how you make it:

Spaghetti con Tonno

Extra-virgin olive oil
1 medium onion, halved and sliced thinly
1 (35-ounce) can whole tomatoes
4 basil leaves
Salt
1 or 2 (12-ounce) cans oil-packed Italian tuna (it depends on how much tuna you like)
1 pound spaghetti (cooked al dente)

- Pour a glug of olive oil into a medium pot, then add the onion. Cook over low heat until the onion softens. Break up the canned tomatoes with your hands or mash them with a fork and add them to the cooked onion. Add the basil leaves and salt to taste. Bring to a boil and cook for a few minutes, then reduce the heat to medium-low. Cover the pot, leaving the lid slightly askew, and simmer for about 20 minutes.

- Add the tuna, replace the lid (askew again), and cook for another 10 minutes. Toss with the spaghetti and serve. The addition of grated cheese is discouraged. Extremely. Actually, just don't do it.

Somehow the combination of tuna, onion, and tomato creates a beautifully sweet sauce that is practically addictive. Matteo devoured his, as did I. Millie did very well, although there was very little tuna in her bowl, and did not even ask for the promised pasta with butter and cheese. I considered it triumph as far as meals with my children go.

June 30

Nico has graduated from Leiths and is now a bona fide chef. I am impressed and proud. I took him to Riva for lunch yet again, where we ate well and drank a wonderful white wine that Mr. Riva had chosen and drank with us. (At this point going to Riva is like walking into another room in our house.) When it was finished, he opened another, mostly because he wanted more, but of course we helped him. When I paid the bill, he told me the gorgeous and not inexpensive wine was on the house. I argued to no avail. A great Italian restaurateur is generosity incarnate.

That evening I had dinner with Colin Firth and Tom Ford at the River Café. I had not seen either of them for a while and it was great fun. We ate pasta and fish. As usual the food was great. What we talked about is none of your business.

Two substantial Italian meals in one day had taken their toll. What was I thinking? How had I scheduled that? I returned home to find Felicity already unpacked and eating some of the string bean minestra I had made for her return and my parents' arrival the next day. Then we went to bed.

July 1

My parents arrived. I was thrilled, as were we all, to see them. I was also relieved. Relief is now just part and parcel of what I feel when I see them. I wish it weren't, but it is. We put Millie on an inflatable mattress in Matteo's room as my father would be sleeping in her room, which is up only *one* flight of stairs, as opposed to the *two* flights leading to the room where my mother is sleeping. Due to a bad knee, climbing stairs is a supreme effort for him and dangerous as well at this point.

It's not much fun watching someone you love age. Especially someone as active and engaged as my father. It's hard because it seems so unfair. It's hard because it's what we all fear. It's hard because we know it's inevitable. It's hard because we know there is no cure for it. But most of all it's hard because it seems unnecessary. Why does it have to happen? Why can't we be like the tortoise and live for over a century without much change? (Maybe the tortoise does change, but it's hard to tell. Has anyone ever said, "I think my tortoise is slowing down"?)

Why can't we be like the yew tree, which has the capacity to live for thousands of years? There's a yew in Scotland that is thought to be five thousand years old, still thriving and growing new shoots. I want everyone I love to be like that tree.

Obviously, I know a life that long isn't possible, but given advances in science, we will soon end up living much longer than we do today. Sadly, I don't think I'll live long enough to find out how long science could have helped me live.

Given that woeful fact, what I would like is the opportunity to remain at a certain age of my choosing for an extended period. Just take a slight pause in the aging process for, let's say, ten to twenty years. I think this is a perfectly reasonable request and someone needs to make it happen.

If that someone is interested, I would choose to remain forty years of age for a decade or so. At forty, one is mature; is experienced in both love and loss, success and failure; is probably not yet in need of eyeglasses; can still awaken in the morning and move through the day without joint pain and muscle aches; and has a memory that is still intact. At forty, one is not old; one has just reached the beginning of middle age and is on the cusp of becoming distinguished.

Anyway, I hope someone figures out how to make this brilliant idea/hope/desire/need of mine a reality for other people, as it's over twenty years too late for me.

My knees are hurting as I sit and write these words.

Why? I'm just sitting.

I rest my case.

Now I'll go rest everything else.

July 2

My mother and Nicolo made meatballs today. As usual she was obsessing about the fat content in the mince (or "ground beef," if you're American). It is my family's belief that the mince needs to have at least 30 percent fat for the meatballs to come out as they should. The highest fat content I have been able to find in a grocery store is 20 percent, at Marks & Spencer. However, the mince from a butcher at our farmers' market seems to have a bit more, so I use that.

Upon perusing the batch of farmers' market mince that I defrosted, my mother was not happy with the look, the smell, nor the feel of it. (This is something she would remind me of many, many times over the next thirty-six hours.) She then told me that M&S has mince with 20 percent fat, and I told her that I was well aware of that fact and assured her that this batch before her was higher in fat, although I did not know the exact percentage. (In England it's difficult to find beef mince with a high fat content because the animals are primarily fed on grass, not on corn, grains, plant husks, and soy like American cattle. British cattle are also not injected with hormones or antibiotics, unlike their US counterparts, which is better for everyone.)

Choosing not to take my word for it, my mother went on a quest to find mince fatty enough for her taste, which resulted in her making several trips to various shops that day. To be fair, she does this between two and four times a day whenever she visits. This is partly because there are an M&S, a Sainsbury's, a butcher, a fishmonger, two bread shops, and three wonderful greengrocers all within walking distance of our home, and besides that, she just loves grocery shopping. Another reason she makes so many mini shopping trips is because without fail she or someone else will have forgotten to buy a certain ingredient. But no matter how many times someone says that they themselves will run out to get the missing piece to that day's culinary puzzle, she refuses and goes herself. This points to what is most likely the *real* reason she makes so many trips to the shops a day: she needs to keep moving.

People nowadays have a multitude of devices that count their daily steps because, the science suggests, the more steps, the better for your health. There is no doubt that is true, but all I can say is that the number of steps my mother takes on any given day, or her mother took, for that matter, would short-circuit every app.

Southern Italians, especially southern Italian women, must possess traces of DNA found in the *Capra aegagrus*, or wild goat. Their indefatigability when it comes to walking up hills and being on their feet for hours on end is mind-boggling. My grandmother had the legs of a twenty-year-old when she passed away at the age of eighty-eight. My mother's legs are the same at the age of eighty-six, but she is not even *close* to the end of her days. In fact, unlike her son, she seems to be reverse aging. How? Why? Genetics. Diet. Metabolism. Yes, of course. But also . . . movement. Movement is life affirming and life extending. As I said, this has been scientifically proven, hence all the step apps. But the irony is that this has been so obvious for centuries. One need not consult a scientist to verify the fact that movement is good for you. One needs only to go grocery shopping with an eighty-six-year-old Calabrese woman and then follow her around the kitchen for just a single day, and one will have proof enough. If you're still standing at the end of that day, you will most likely have a very long life.

Eventually my mother made the meatballs, with Nico's assistance. I steered clear. Too many cooks and all that. Yet, as I busied myself with other tasks, I overheard their discussions, comments, moans, and so on about what bread they should use (besides the mince, bread is the most crucial ingredient to a good meatball) and stages of its staleness; amounts of garlic, cheese, parsley, eggs, and salt; and of course that old chestnut, fat content.

Whatever ratio of ingredients they ended up using, the result was delicious. The only problem was that because the meatballs were made the day before they were to be eaten, my older children pilfered so many that evening that there were just barely enough to go around the next day. In the future, I'm putting them into a refrigerated lockbox.

The next day, when we ate them, my parents complained a bit more about the insubstantial amount of fat as well as the flavor of the beef itself, which they found "too meaty." I honestly can't say they were wrong, but sometimes we must let things go.

July 5

We had the War Child dinner at Riva. This was the menu:

Prosciutto e melone

Fried zucchini flowers stuffed with mozzarella and anchovies

Grilled langoustine

Mixed grilled vegetables

Risotto alla Norma

Bistecca tagliata

You will notice that often the same recipes crop up a lot within these pages. The reason is that they are classic Italian seasonal dishes that are relatively easy for a restaurant or a home cook to prepare for many people. (Except for the *risotto alla Norma*, which is easier if it is made with pasta because the pasta is simpler to cook for a larger group.) These dishes are also recognizable to many diners and for the most part suit all tastes, and dietary needs and wants. Plus, they're really good. Mr. Riva and his staff served our large table of twenty-two with their usual effortless grace. More important, we reached our goal of raising one hundred thousand pounds for a vital charity at a crucial time. When isn't it a crucial time for a charity such as this? Sadly, there's always a war somewhere.

July 10

Fee and I went to Paris by train (the only way to travel as far as I am concerned) to visit Emily, John, and my publicist Jenn. They were there for the French premiere of *Oppenheimer*. John had kindly and generously organized a private tour of the Musée d'Orsay, which was thrilling. I had not been in there for a long time and had forgotten how many impressionist treasures it holds. Afterward we stopped at a famous art shop and bought some supplies.

As I love to draw, whenever I travel, I always bring art supplies with me. The longer my stay, the more I bring. If I come across an art supply store on my travels, I can't help but go in and purchase something. My father taught my sisters and me to not only *look* at the world but to really *see* it, and, if the spirit moved us, to capture it in whatever medium we chose. He was always pointing out the details of a tree, a stone, the sky, or the light and how it touches things and shapes things, and how the shapes of those things seem to become other things, or that the heart of an artichoke is a marvel, or that the inside of a beet is something beautiful and resembles the rings of a tree, and when that beet is cooked and put on a plate, coated in olive oil, a splash of red-wine vinegar, a little salt, and some oregano, not only does it taste sublime, but the quasi-psychedelic colored liquid that is created by those ingredients is a magnificent thing. Looking at something for just that little bit longer than you might normally will change not only the way you see that thing but everything else thereafter. That's why he was and still is a great teacher.

We made our way back to the hotel, had a bit of wine, and then headed for the banks of the Seine. A riverboat was our destination because Universal Pictures was throwing a party for those involved in the film and hangers-on like me and Felicity. On the boat were a few people I had worked with over the years, and I finally got to meet Robert Downey Jr., of whom I am a huge fan. He is everything Emily said he was, brilliantly funny, charming, and more than nice.

A rather formal sit-down dinner was served as the boat eased its way up and down the Seine. The event was lovely. The food was not.

Watermelon gazpacho was the first course. After I tasted it, I feared the second course of rolled beef slathered in a green paste would be just as unnecessarily fussy and strange, so I opted out.

I ate a piece of bread, sipped white wine, and attempted to chat with Cillian Murphy but was too starstruck to form proper sentences.

July 12

Emily, Jenn, my new best friend Robert D. Jr., and Robert's agent Phil came for dinner. All my kids were there as well as my parents and Lottie. The list of guests had grown throughout the day, so I needed to keep adjusting the menu. I had intended to make a risotto with peas and asparagus, but as the numbers grew, I opted for pasta with onions and a bit of garlic, peas, butter, and Parmigiano. Making risotto for that many people can be difficult, and meat or a meat-based sauce was out of the question, as Robert is not a meat eater and Felicity and I always defer to the vegetarian or pescatarian at the table. Vegans are harder to cater to if there is a large group of people, but usually we can make one or two dishes to satisfy the strict requirements of that diet.

I must admit that I grapple with the idea of veganism. I can understand abiding by it for health reasons (a friend of mine did it for a while to relieve inflammation from injuries due to many years of sports and stunt work), as well as a way of proactively supporting sustainability, but selfishly I know I would struggle with the incredibly limited culinary options available, especially when traveling. I believe that eating everything in moderation is the key. Life is so short and tasting food of all kinds brings me such joy that I could never be so dogmatic, but it is an admirable choice if it suits one.

Earlier in the day, my mom and I had visited the fishmonger and bought two large filets of cod (which she insisted on paying for), as I wanted to make *cod alla livornese*.

I made the pasta and the cod with the help of many, and we ate and chatted and drank wine, and I thought how lucky I was to have all these funny, ridiculously talented people whom I admire so much at our table and to have them get to know, if even briefly, the people I admire most, my parents.

The British film and television industry has been growing in leaps and bounds over the last decade and a half. Studios are being expanded and new ones built in and around London because it's often less expensive for American producers to make shows and films here due to tax breaks, as well as because of the extraordinary talent pool in front of and behind the camera. I feel fortunate that my moving to London coincided with this boom, not only because I get to work on a wide variety of projects and sleep in my own bed every night, but because many of my friends who are based in America often come here to work for extended periods of time.

This has caused our house to become a home away from home for the gypsies of the celluloid world. Felicity and I love hosting friends from "across the pond" because we get to spend private and uninterrupted time with each other, and they get a respite from eating in restaurants or ordering room service night after night.

Actors are at once the moth and the flame. They will seek out each other's company and find instant camaraderie in the commonality of their peripatetic lifestyles and experiences. Most people, especially men, do not make friends quickly, and it can take years once they do for them to be open, honest, and vulnerable with each other. But for the most part actors are different. It is an innate aspect of the actor's psyche to form relationships quickly, partly because it's an essential requirement of the job.

Good morning, Actor X, this is Actor Y, who's playing your wife. We're going to start with scene number zero, where you've just come out of the shower, you confront her about the affair, and she seduces you and then tries to kill you. Or vice versa.

Because actors might be away from home for long periods of time, finding each other after work for drinks, a meal, or an excursion on a day off is vital to staving off loneliness, and getting to know each other swiftly makes all those things easier. The intensity of filming emotionally charged scenes at all hours for weeks or months at a time, often in miserable weather in the middle of nowhere, speeds up the metabolic rate of friendships for actors, if only to allow for a sympathetic ear that will listen to endless rantings about the work hours, the rain, the accommodations, the caterer, the director, or (and yes, it does happen) even a fellow actor. Our home has become a kind of sanctuary for those bleary-eyed thespians who have wandered to London to find or maintain their fame and fortune. And we're glad when they do.

July 13

Took my parents to the Paul McCartney photo exhibit at the newly renovated National Portrait Gallery that I saw a few weeks ago in preparation for the interview I did with him. I was quite nervous, but Paul is so easy to talk to that it went smoothly and will forever be a highlight of my life. That is obviously an understatement.

As we went through the exhibit and I was pushing my dad in a wheelchair, I noticed that he was barely engaged and kept nodding off. He'd been sleeping a lot since he'd arrived, had seemed a bit removed, was having difficulty thinking of words and slurring his speech. When we got home, I asked my mother if she had noticed these things and she said she had. I suggested that he might have had a mini stroke and perhaps we should get him checked. She agreed. I was afraid. My father is as active as a man with one very bad knee can be at the age of ninety-three. He still has all his mental faculties, still makes jewelry in a little shop on their porch, still sketches, still does calligraphy, and is sous chef to my indefatigable, brilliant cook of a mother. So, to see him like that caused me to imagine a host of unpleasant scenarios that might unfold over the next few days

After a doctor assessed him at our home, we admitted him to a hospital, where he was seen by a doctor who specializes in acute medicine. This basically means he's a doctor who specializes in figuring out what's wrong with you when nobody else can. After two days and a battery of tests, he posited that some of my father's medication might be causing these strokelike symptoms as well as the tiredness, because they were interfering with his diastolic blood pressure. After removing two supplements and two medications, the next day my father was practically back to his old, but not *as old*, self. In short, he had been overmedicated by his doctors, which is not uncommon in the States, especially when it comes to the elderly. It was fascinating to see that what the doctor had suggested almost immediately resulted in the positive outcome we'd hoped for. We were all very much relieved. As they say, hope for the best but expect the worst. This time the best happened.

What was equally fascinating but not nearly as positive was the small, sad lobby café in this brand-new state-of-the-art hospital. On the counter by the till sat a plethora of cakes, muffins, cookies, and other sugar-filled misfirings of the snack world. Behind that was a counter on which sat rows of baskets filled with bag upon small bag of fried, popped, or baked chips and crisps of every ilk, from corn to lentil to potato, to rice, to carrot, to vegetable, to probably birchbark. Bag after bag after bag, ad nauseam.

Opposite that high-sodium display sat a small fridge that held paltry amounts of tuna and egg salad stuffed between slices of bloated bread masquerading as "sandwiches," a couple of fading falafel wraps, and a lone gluten-free veggie wrap. To add insult to injury, the coffee was dreadful.

I bought a sandwich and found it foul. My mother refused to eat anything. (She can go for extended periods of time eating little or nothing, like a navy SEAL or a camel). The hospital food served to patients was a bit better than that of most hospitals but still not acceptable, especially to my father's palate.

Why is it that when people are doing all they can to keep you healthy or even *save your life*, they undermine their heroic efforts by giving you awful food? This is a question every head of every hospital should ask themselves. School boards might want to have a think about that as well.

Anyway, Saturday morning my father was discharged, and we headed back to our house, where he shaved, showered, and settled in front of the television to watch the Wimbledon men's doubles final. That afternoon the kitchen was abuzz with activity that culminated in a wonderful meal with the entire family, including my very awake father. Felicity and my mother had prepared homemade gnocchi because it pleases everyone and goes with so many sauces. Nicolo made a fresh tomato sauce with a bit of lobster. We drank red and white wine and feasted on a meal fit for a ninety-three-year-old patriarch and his family. Although I knew this would not be the last time something like this would happen, I was relieved and happy to see him and my mother enjoying themselves at the table. It is where they belong, because it is where they are most happy.

July 16–17

Felicity and I went to the Newt, a stunning place in Somerset that covers countless acres and has a working farm, three restaurants, and beautiful hotel rooms integrated tastefully in renovated outbuildings. We never wanted to leave. The food, mostly vegetarian, culled from their many gardens, was sublime and made one forget about meat at all. A roasted onion with a crispy exterior and a soft interior resembled a deep-fried artichoke. *Hangop* (homemade strained yogurt) with thick sourdough bread was addictive. The zucchini with aioli was extraordinary, and the pork belly (which we almost always order because we love it so) was fatty and perfectly crackled, but we only tasted it because as usual we had overordered. We ate lunch there both days, overlooking one of the magnificent gardens.

As I sat down to eat on the second day, an older gentleman came up and told me how much he had enjoyed *Searching for Italy* and that he and his wife were big fans. He then told me that his wife had passed away not long ago, that she would have been very excited to meet me and how he wished she could be there in this moment.

His hands shook a bit when he took mine, to which he held on tightly. I recognized that the shaking was from age as well as nervousness, but I also knew that it was brought about by a flood of emotion.

When he spoke of his late wife, I knew instantly that he carried her and all her feelings inside of him. Because she was no longer there, *he* had become the conduit through which she could still experience the world and through which the world could still experience her.

When someone you love dies, you absorb them. You take on their feelings and simultaneously experience life through their eyes and their heart as well as your own. In essence, you become them. This is not a conscious choice. It just happens. And it happens because one is not yet fully capable of accepting that person's absence. It keeps them alive. Or at least it makes them less dead.

I wanted to hug him when I expressed my condolences, but I didn't. Perhaps I thought it might be too much for both of us.

As he held my hand, I knew that the very real and visceral feeling of her presence brought about by this moment, an experience they would have shared were she still alive, would wane over time. But he could not know this then, nor did he need to. That realization or knowledge was years ahead of him. Yet her presence at times such as these would never disappear completely. It would always be there. Always. But soon, it would become less prevalent. In time her presence would slip into his body, his heart, and his thoughts, sometimes gently, sometimes joltingly, but it would never last for as long as it would today. Eventually, years from now, it would alight on the tip of his soul for just a second or two, carrying with it a shiver of the past and a glimpse of a future that might have been.

And then it would disappear once again.

As I was leaving, he stopped me and asked if I would ever write a cookbook for bereaved spouses. Not knowing what to say, I told him about the cookbook that Felicity and I had written and explained that the recipes were straightforward, and that he might enjoy it. Then he asked if it contained any recipes for one.

July 18

Matteo is obsessed with football, also known as soccer. Pictures of contemporary soccer greats cut from newspapers are plastered all over his bedroom walls. Most of them are of his hero, Harry Kane, who played for Tottenham and has now moved to Bayern Munich. Pelé has made the grade as well. I had shown Matteo videos of Pelé and told him what a brilliant player he had been and that I had been lucky enough to see him play with the New York Cosmos in the late seventies. I had gone to the game at Shea Stadium with teammates from my high school soccer team. As far as I can remember, we were very lucky to get tickets because it was to be Pelé's last game ever.

The place was packed and even Muhammed Ali was in attendance, seated not far from us. At one point Ali left his seat and headed up into the stadium corridor. One of my teammates convinced me to follow him so he could take a picture—I guess he had a camera—and so we did. The boxer made his way into the bathroom with a bodyguard close by. We followed stealthily and then stood at the doorway and stared at the back of him as he relieved himself like any another man would do at a urinal. As I was telling my friend that I wanted to return to our seats, I heard a roar from the crowd that was deafening. We sprinted back only to discover that Pelé had just scored. I felt ill. Not only had my soccer hero just scored and I had missed it, but it turned out that it was the last professional goal he would ever score. I missed "The Greatest of All Time" score the final goal of his career just so I could watch the other

"The Greatest" urinate. If ever I take Matteo to see Harry Kane play, neither of us will be leaving our seat, no matter which famous bladder calls out for relief.

Anyway, I'm thrilled about his love of the beautiful game. Every other day he tells me he's going to be a professional footballer. And every *other* other day he tells me he wants to be a herpetologist. And on all those days I believe him and hope both dreams come true.

Made mushroom risotto for me and Felicity. It turned out very well. So much easier to make it for just two people. I wanted to put saffron in it to make it a proper *risotto milanese*, but I know Felicity doesn't care for it. *Risotto milanese* was one of my favorite things that my mother made when I was a kid. She knew exactly how much saffron with which to flavor it. If you put in too much of it the rice becomes bitter, hence Felicity's resistance. Meaning I probably put too much. Whenever I'm in Milan it is the first thing I order. It's usually made without mushrooms, but I happen to love it with them. Risotto is such a delicate and temperamental thing. It takes the patience of a saint to make it, and significant concentration as well. There really is an art to making it well, which I have yet to master, although I am getting better all the time. But in the end, I know that risotto is an elusive, coy little beast that will forever remain untamed.

An Evening in July (the Date Is Vague)

One sunny early-summer evening Felicity and I were cooking as usual, and I decided to slice a bunch of zucchini to grill on the barbecue. I'm not always a fan of grilled vegetables but these were rather large and would not have been good to sauté as they would have been too watery, and I didn't have the energy to bake them *alla parmigiana*. So, I marinated them, fired up the barbecue, and threw them on, and of course some fell through the grate, which really annoyed me. (For some reason I never remember to buy something that will prevent this.) Eventually, I finally get the rest of the zucchini onto the barbecue without mishap, when the doorbell rings. Felicity says she's not answering it because she's busy, and besides, she *always* answers it and would *I* mind answering it. Begrudgingly I go to answer it but neglect to first look at the video monitor and see who it is.

I open the door and before me stands a consciously disheveled, fairly good-looking man in his late forties or so wearing a Barbour jacket and Wellington boots and holding two dogs, at the end of well-worn leashes, of some breed that people who dress like he does transport everywhere they go. He introduces himself in what I instantly recognize as a posh accent and tells me that he is on the board of a charity that supports bereaved children of deceased parents.

I feel a pang of pain in my heart just hearing those words. He then tells me that he knows that my children have a deceased parent.

Another, deeper pang.

He then asks, given my and my children's experience, if I wouldn't want to participate in his charity by hosting an event like the renowned actor so-and-so and the illustrious multihyphenate so-and-so have done in the past.

After a few more famous names drop from his mouth onto my threshold, I stammer for a moment, probably because I'm intimidated by his upper-crustiness but also because I don't know how to respond, because I'm starting to feel a bit ill from the surge of deep-rooted emotional memories as well as somewhat uneasy about this whole exchange.

Then, for some unknown reason, I suddenly apologize for not inviting him in and explain that I'm in the middle of cooking and besides, our cats might not take kindly to his hounds and vice versa. He says he understands and then tells me some more about his charity and then I tell him that if he emails my assistant and sends me all the pertinent information, I will have a look at it. I write down the email for him and he thanks me, and I close the door and head back to the barbecue.

The barbecue that I left on high.

The barbecue that now holds the charred remains of my painstakingly sliced and gently marinated zucchini.

I'm furious.

I shout a lot.

I curse the posh man.

And his dogs.

And the angrier I get about the devastation his visit has wrought upon my supper, the angrier I get about his gall and the inappropriateness of his visit and how much it has unsettled me.

Let me make it clear that the charity this fellow described sounded like a necessary and worthy one. As I have made evident, I am a supporter of several charities and do what I can to raise awareness and money for them as well as make financial donations myself. I receive requests to support a new charity practically every month, but trying to work with all of them would be spreading myself too thin and take away from the impact I can have on the others. However, those requests are almost always via email or letter.

But what kind of person, may I ask, decides to knock on someone's door unannounced on a Saturday evening between cocktail hour and dinnertime and ask them for a favor related to the most painful time in their life?

Has he never heard of letter writing? That age-old tradition of putting pen to paper, writing a request on that paper, placing that paper into an envelope, licking the envelope, sealing it, addressing it (the latter action easily done because he *obviously has my address!*), licking a stamp, sticking it in the upper right-hand corner of the envelope, and popping the whole kit and caboodle into one of the many red cast-iron Royal Mail boxes that sit conveniently on countless London street corners.

I mean, really? *I* hesitate to go to my neighbors, with whom I am friendly, and ask to borrow a cup of sugar! What did this guy expect when he knocked on my door? Did he expect me to say, *Oh, hello, Mr. Poshwhoeverthefuckyouare, I was hoping you'd pop by on a Saturday evening while I'm enjoying some much-needed quality time with my family and bring up my dead wife and my older children's pain and grief, because I hadn't thought about any of those things enough this week!*

And on top of it all he turned my zucchini to dust.

A few days later Lottie received a very long email about the charity, which, as I said, is a noble one, but in a subsequent email exchange he was very offended when she suggested that it was inappropriate of him to come to my home.

He was the one who was offended!

Really!?

I made a donation.

July 20

Went to Jilly Cooper's summer party at her Cotswolds home and met more of the folks working on the production of *Rivals* that Felicity is producing. There was only finger food, based on finger food that would have been eaten at such a fête in the 1980s, when the show takes place. There were plates of whole pineapples skewered with other fruit and tiny quiches and things that looked like they may have been kept in a deep freeze since the eighties and defrosted for just this occasion. All I can say is that I'm glad food tastes have changed since then. Jilly was as gracious as ever, still standing and chatting vivaciously when we departed, which is a miracle for someone who has basically lived on mayonnaise and champagne for eighty-six years.

July 21

Took the train home this morning after an okay breakfast at the hotel.

Got home famished. Made a ham, cheese, mustard, and tomato toastie (known as a grilled sandwich in America). Had it with a beer. F . . . ing great.

Made sausage, rice, and green beans for the kids. Millie is in the last stages of chicken pox and isn't very happy. She asked for pasta with butter and cheese, and I could not say no. She is very brave.

Made fettucine with peas, onion, *guanciale*, string beans, and fresh tomato for me. It was okay. Not great. Should have cooked the *guanciale*, peas, and beans more and should have put the tomatoes through a Foley mill because the skins were tough. Next time.

Felicity arrived home after navigating her way through train cancellations, which happens far too often here, and ate some string bean minestra. I, of course, ate again with her. I finished the gazpacho I had made a couple of days before. A José Andrés recipe that is delicious and so simple to make. What a brilliant chef he is. I love gazpacho. Could eat it every day.

July 22

I took Matteo to the farmers' market. He devoured a sausage and bacon sandwich while I overbought vegetables and meat. We went to the hardware store to buy sandpaper so I could finish sanding and stripping the outdoor teak furniture that was incorrectly coated with varnish and is now peeling and looking awful. It was done last year when I was away working, so I wasn't here to say, *Oh, could you please not do that?*

Hayley Atwell and her fiancée, Ned, came over for lunch. Felicity made a great Greek salad and we picked at pre-prepared goodies, cheese, and olives that Matteo and I bought at the market.

July 23

Lately, Matteo has been obsessing about snakes and snake traps. I helped him make a snake trap out of a plastic container and a plastic water bottle. He is quite ingenious, I have to say. It is based on a fish trap he saw made on YouTube. Once we made it, he began to obsess about what bait he should use and where and how to get that bait. Felicity and I suggested rodents and insects but also told him there probably weren't a lot of snakes in our garden. He refused to believe that that might be true. He remains intent on catching an adder. I remain intent on his not.

To indulge his serpentine fixation, we surfed snake-devoted websites and came across a video, again on YouTube, of a man in a jungle somewhere, who was obviously indigenous to that jungle, cooking and then eating a basket of small snakes. We could not help but watch it.

First, he poached them briefly in a pan of water that was boiling over a small fire, and then he scraped off their scales with a spoon. Then he tied them in knots—not sure why—fried them in lots of oil, and added sliced ginger, lemongrass, and possibly curry leaves. (The video has no voiceover, and he never says a word, so some ingredients are a mystery. He just cooks with great intent, and all you hear is the sound of the fire and the sizzling oil.) He then covered the pan with a woven bamboo lid.

In a mortar and pestle he ground lots of garlic, chili, lime juice, and maybe some vinegar (but it could have been some kind of wine) into a sauce of sorts. At this point he returned to the pan, and the snakes were fried to a crisp. He placed them onto a large leaf and proceeded to eat them ravenously with his hands as he dipped them into the chili sauce.

I am as repelled and terrified of snakes as Matteo is fascinated and enamored with them, but *both* of us were cringing through the whole video at just the thought of eating what this fellow was eating. And yet, we were mesmerized. We could not stop watching it. This man was so assured about his preparation and cooking of the snakes and so loved eating them that it "normalized" it for us. (I know I sound like an "ugly American.")

He needed protein. Snakes are animals with a lot of protein, and they were available to him. So, he caught some. This method of preparing them was most likely passed down to him from his ancestors, so he prepared them that way and then he ate them. Were he to see how *we* raise or procure, prepare, and eat whatever animals we choose to eat, I am sure he would be cringing even more than we did.

Snakes are eaten all over the world. To me a snake is a frightening creature.

To Matteo a snake is a dream pet.

To the man in the video the snake was sustenance made very edible.

It's one of the best cooking videos I've ever seen. No music. No commentary. No text at the bottom of the frame. Only ambient sounds of the environment, the crackling of the oil in the pan, and a man crunching his way through a feast of snakes.

Anyway, our viewing caused Matteo to think about snakes even more, if that's possible, to the point where by the end of Sunday afternoon I had to firmly insist that he not bring them up at least until the next morning because I was losing my mind. He took it very well.

The moratorium lasted about thirty minutes, until he slithered his way back into the topic once more. I must set a trap.

July 27

Took the kids to an indoor trampoline park, which was the loudest place on earth. They jumped for over an hour while Felicity and I somehow got work done on our laptops. Millie got a bloody nose (like her mother, she is prone to them) because someone elbowed her. She cried for a moment and then quickly bounded back into the fray. Seconds later, Felicity was rubbing furiously to remove Millie's nose blood from the new winter-white cashmere cardigan I had just bought for her two days before. I tried not to look.

Although we had brought our own sandwiches, we ordered the kids hot dogs, which they devoured, and chips, most of which Felicity and I devoured because they were great. We are definitely returning to the trampoline park, but next time we'll be packing nose guards, bloodproof clothing, and earplugs.

Afterward we went to Garsons farm, about ten minutes away, where you can pick your own vegetables, fruit, and flowers. We picked French beans, sunflowers, sweet corn, red currants, and blackberries. The kids were in heaven as they are obsessed with the latter two fruits, especially blackberries. Fortunately, blackberry bushes grow wild all over England. They are the sweetest weed.

Spaghettini with puréed marinara sauce was our dinner. Felicity wanted to purée the marinara to see if Millie would eat it more readily. She didn't. But we did.

Also had a side of rainbow chard I had made a couple of days before. Here's how I make it:

Rainbow Chard

2 large bunches rainbow chard (or any chard)
Salt
1 clove garlic, halved
Extra-virgin olive oil

- Strip the chard leaves from the stems. Wash and soak the leaves in cold water. Roughly chop the stems. Wash and soak them in cold water for a few minutes, then rinse.
- Put the chopped stems in a large, deep frying pan and cover them with water; add a good pinch of salt and the garlic. Put a lid on the pan and bring to a boil. Then lower the heat to medium and cook for about 10 minutes.
- Rinse the chard leaves and chop them roughly. Add them to the pan and cover them with water. Add a bit more salt, put the lid back on, and cook until wilted and soft, about 10 minutes.
- Strain all the liquid, place the chard on a platter, and drizzle it with extra-virgin olive oil.

Note: A half cup or so of marinara or passata can be added to this, as well as a pinch of red pepper flakes. You could also toss this with a pasta of your choice (nothing too small) and serve it with grated ricotta salata, pecorino, or Parmigiano-Reggiano.

I make this just about every week. Part of the beauty of a certain dish or a meal is that it is ephemeral. It can be repeated but it will never be the same. Like the performance of a play. The lines and staging will be the same, but the result will always be a little different. Always the same but different.

July 28

Dinner at Sabor with the wonderful writer and brilliant host of the podcast *How to Fail*, Elizabeth Day, and her husband, Justin Basini. We became friends a few years ago for several reasons but I think mostly because we are all food obsessives. I really don't know what to say about the restaurant, Sabor. I've eaten there countless times and it is consistently brilliant. Nieves Barragan is the chef/owner and was awarded a Michelin star a couple of years back. She was the head chef at a Barrafina before giving all of us in London the gift of her distinctive take on Spanish cuisine when she opened Sabor. However, the place is not precious or fussy in the way "starry" restaurants can be. The menu is Nieves's take on Spanish tapas and then some. In short, it's one of the best restaurants I've ever been to, and she is one of the nicest people one could ever meet. I'm starving just thinking about it. And I just ate.

July 29

Went to the farmers' market with my daughter Camilla, who is back for the summer (finally!!), and the younger kids. Bought them sausage sandwiches, which they ate while I bought far too much of everything that follows:

Zucchini

Zucchini flowers

Beef mince

Heirloom tomatoes

Baby celery (never seen it before)

Parsley root (never seen it before—looked like skinny parsnips)

Broccoli

Eggplant

Cauliflower

Marrow bones

Onions

Spring onions that tasted more like garlic, but they weren't ramps (never seen them before)

Parsley

Stuffed grape leaves

Nocellara olives

2 Spanish tortillas

2 containers of gazpacho

1 baguette

1 ciabatta

Got home and ate the tortilla and gazpacho. Also discovered that Matteo now has chicken pox just as Millie's spots are drying up and disappearing. His case seems milder, however, and he is in good spirits. Fingers crossed it doesn't worsen. Unpacked the spoils of the market and began to cook what is below:

Me

Big pot of chili con carne

Felicity

Roasted carrots and parsley root

Potatoes and artichokes in a broth

We ate some of each dish throughout the day.

July 30

We cooked again.

Me

Eggplant parmigiana

Rabbit with carrots, celery, tomatoes, white wine, and Taggiasca olives

Felicity

Chive aioli

Sea bass carpaccio with tomato, olive oil, and lemon

Tomato salad

We had friends for dinner that night, and in deference to the non–meat eater we served a vegetarian meal, except for the carpaccio, comprised of the dishes we had cooked over the last two days. I saved the chili con carne and the rabbit for the coming week.

I had tasted the chili again that morning alongside the leftover tortilla. It was my deservedly hearty breakfast after cleaning up the garden and continuing to strip the varnish off the handsome outdoor furniture that was made ugly by the varnishing zealot.

The chili was delish, but I'm not sure why. This is the reason I will never be a great cook. I never measure anything. I almost always judge every phase of a dish by my eyes, my nose, and my mouth. I hate measuring things. This is most likely because I am numerically handicapped or am afflicted by what is properly known as dyscalculia. Therefore, measuring, or, God forbid, *converting measurements*, is a form of slow torture. (I will confess that for this reason writing cookbooks and recipes is not the easiest.) I also tasted the rabbit. I thought that was delish as well. Again, why? I have no idea. It may well be that I was just delirious from the fumes of the toxic varnish-stripping gel I was using and at that point would have thought anything was delish. Maybe I should inhale that stuff more often. It takes away all self-doubt and judgment about my cooking.

July 31

I can't stop thinking about the guy eating the snakes in that video. The sound of crunching and his concentration as he ate them.

Thankfully Matteo's chicken pox is on the wane. We have decided to buy him a green anole, which is a small lizard about the size of a chameleon. He has been haranguing us for so long about buying him some sort of reptile that we have finally acquiesced. It is an innocuous little light green creature with a purple dewlap that expands when it feels threatened. I wish I had a dewlap like that. When Matteo heard this news, it seemed to have assuaged at least some of the pain of the pox.

We've ordered the necessary vertical terrarium, or "vivarium," which we must first outfit with plants, a climbing structure, lights, and a thermometer because it must be set up and brought to the correct temperature before the little fella can call it home. Matteo is beside himself with excitement. I'm sure the cats will be beside the terrarium with excitement.

Well, as the old saying goes, one man's pet is another pet's meal.

August 3

Matteo's bout with chicken pox is over. Only the scabs remain, which he is very good about not scratching. His outbreak was worse than Millie's, poor fellow. But now he's back to running around like a lunatic. Thank God.

Richard Madden and Cheryl came for dinner. My eldest daughter, Isabel, and Lottie came as well. A bit of a reunion of the *Citadel* Junketeers. I made tagliatelle with raw tomatoes that had been marinated in EVOO, garlic, and basil in the fridge. After a couple of hours, I brought them to room temperature, added coarse salt, cooked the pasta, and tossed it all together. The heat of the pasta gently "cooks" the mixture; a dollop of soft goat's cheese mixed in and a sprinkling of Parmigiano make it impossibly good. Best made in the summer when tomatoes are in season and very ripe. Larger tomatoes work better than cherry tomatoes.

For the main I fried two rib eye steaks and two sirloins and served them with a room-temperature green sauce made with parsley, rosemary, and spring onion, as well as a few of those garlic/onion things I bought at the farmers' market last week, thyme, EVOO, lemon juice, and lemon zest. Also made a compound butter with shallots, parsley, and garlic. Neglected to make a side or a salad. But everyone was very happy. Even me.

August 5

Did not go to the farmers' market, which always makes me a bit sad and slightly disconnected from where we live. Even if it's the same purveyors every week, selling basically the same things, I take great comfort in going to the market. We all know that it's the small consistencies of life that are vital to keeping us grounded. Farmers' markets ground us but also remind us, for better or worse, of the passage of time. Spring and its greens, summer and its tomatoes, autumn and its squash, winter and its black kale subtly guide us through another year.

That afternoon we had lunch at our friends Dominic and Paul's house in Bray, a little town about thirty miles west of London. Dom made a Bolognese. I don't know what the hell he did but it was f—ing great. Sadly, we used an inferior brand of tagliatelle, which fell apart as I stirred it in the pot. It was unworthy of his sauce. I remember buying cheap pasta when I had my apartment on campus during my senior year of college. I told my parents that I had bought the supermarket brand because it was inexpensive. Their response was something like, "What?! No! Don't do that! You have to buy a good pasta. We'll give you more money if you need it!"

I never bought the supermarket brand again.

Came home and made sausages, corn, peas, and pasta with cheese for the kids for dinner. Fee and I did not eat.

Speaking of corn, the ears of corn we picked last week at Garsons farm were delicious. The best I've ever had in the UK. Usually it's awful. Dense, dark yellow kernels that are more bitter than sweet. But this was reminiscent of the New York State summer corn that I grew up with. Must find out why.

August 6

I made lentils, which I mistakenly overcooked (because I was helping Matteo make a "raft" out of bamboo sticks), but they were still good. Also made *pasta fagioli* with just cannellini beans but it needed borlotti beans, which I forgot to use. What is happening to me? I'm very unfocused. Still distressed because Fee and I had an argument and I feel awful. Ugh. I stripped and sanded another piece of outdoor furniture of its undignified and unnecessary coat of varnish.

Colin Firth came over for dinner tonight. He was an hour and a half late because he thought he was to come the next night. But I am hardly one to talk. My memory gets worse every day. He needs someone like Lottie. She helps me remember the when, the where, and sometimes even the *why* of anything I'm doing. It could be my age, but I think it's because my mind is often elsewhere rather than in the moment. For example, when I'm introduced to someone, I have a tendency to focus too much on their features (eyes, teeth, skin, nose, moles, hair, etc.), their voice, their clothing, their behavior, and then I instantly imagine them as children or at home eating, and then what their home looks like and how clean it is or isn't, and then I imagine whether they have a spouse or a partner and what *that* person might look like and how they met and whether they're affectionate with each other and happy together, whether they have children, and if they do, who puts the kids to bed, and then, and then, and then, and then, and then, and then I forget just about every single word they've said. It's exhausting. Most men won't ask for directions because they see the inability to find one's way as a failure of sorts. I have no problem asking for directions but hesitate only because once I encounter the person of whom I'm asking the directions, what I just described above happens and then I become more lost in my idea of their life than I am lost geographically. It's also the reason I never remember anyone's name, only their face.

People are always amazed by how actors can remember their lines. I think most actors are often amazed that nonactors can remember everything else. Again, I must quote from Tom Stoppard's *Rosencrantz and Guildenstern Are Dead*. The character of the Player says, "We're actors. We're the opposite of people." He's not wrong.

I hadn't seen Colin for a while and had missed him. Felicity made ribs and I overcooked some potatoes, and we had a couple of salads. All good except for my potatoes.

August 7

Exercised while watching some of the quarterfinal of the World Cup women's football. England vs. Nigeria. Great game. Had to shut it off during the second overtime because I had things to do and it was becoming so stressful. England was playing with only ten players due to a red card. Saw later that day that England won in a shootout. I cannot bear to watch shootouts. I hate them. Glad the Lionesses won.

Ate one scrambled egg for breakfast on a piece of focaccia. Got the kids from tennis camp. Took Matteo to the local park so he could try to catch tiny fish with a net in the semipolluted stream. Afterward we went for lunch. For him, fried goujons and chips. For me, a beer and a goat cheese and pepper tart. Bit spongy. Fish and chips were delish. Then I took him for a much-needed haircut.

As his gorgeous curly locks fell to the floor, they revealed a face that has changed so much since we last took him there not that long ago. I was not prepared for it. It is all happening too quickly, and I don't like it. Every day they are changing, but you don't see it until suddenly one moment you do. And then you feel like you missed something. But you didn't. You were right there. It was just imperceptible. It's the reason we mark our children's heights on a wall, just to have a record of their growth. If we don't have this physical/visual record to refer to, suddenly one day we're shocked to find them bending down to kiss us goodbye.

August 8

Had our friend Rich over for dinner to celebrate Felicity's birthday. They have been colleagues for years and he is also Matteo's godfather. The risotto was some of the best I've ever made (he said, tooting his own horn). I use Acquerello rice, which is hard to overcook and therefore also hard to cook properly, so I never quite get it right. This time I tried something different. After about twenty minutes I decided to lower the heat a bit and cover it, which is not something you ever do with risotto. A few minutes later I tasted it, and it had the exact amount of firmness I wanted. I took it off the heat, stirred in a few knobs of cold butter and two handfuls of Parmigiano, covered it, and let it sit for a minute or two. This is what is known as "*mantecato*," or the adding of fat, hence the butter and cheese. Felicity loved it, as did I.

The baked chicken was a bit overcooked but not bad.

August 9

Felicity opened her presents (luckily, she liked them) and we exercised, then went to Garsons farm with the kids. Camilla came with us as we won't be seeing her again before she leaves to go back to school in Idaho. We are all sad about that, but she will be back for Christmas. We picked apples, raspberries, plums, and of course more wild blackberries. The weather has finally taken a turn for the better, meaning it's not a rainy, chilly, autumnlike day as is usual in August, and the kids were so happy to be picking fruit in the sunshine. We literally had to drag Millie away from the raspberry bushes as she yelled, "*I just can't stop picking them!*"

Dropped the kids at my in-laws', then Felicity and Camilla and I went home and made chicken salad with the leftovers from the night before. It was slightly anemic. We had forgotten to add chives, which give it a lift. Then we headed to Paddington station for a *Rivals* party in Bristol.

I love train travel. Especially in England and Europe. So relaxing. Wish we could travel through Italy by train when we film the show but logistically it's impossible. So, it's cars.

But I'm not a car person. If I never got into one again it would be too soon, because quite simply, I can't sit still for very long. I prefer train travel over car, boat, and certainly plane travel. I have no fear of flying, I just find it soul sucking. Boats are fine, on calm seas, because being on the water is like being in a new world. But ultimately, for me, travel is best by train. I can stretch my legs, pace the aisle, read a book, sketch, write, eat, go to the bar car, or just take in the scenery. In the end, when it comes to automobiles, I suppose the only thing that attracts me is the aesthetics of certain makes. Land Rover Defenders (old ones), Raymond Loewy's Avanti, the 1940s Willys jeep, vintage Volkswagen Beetles and vans, a silver 1960s Jaguar, a boxy '70s Volvo, and a '70s Citroën DS 20, the last three all owned at some point by my uncle Bob and aunt Dora.

In Bristol we went to a place called Rick's. Very nice staff who made proper cocktails. We tasted a few and ate some oysters and other nibbles. They were wonderful bartenders who just want to keep learning more and inventing new drinks. How nice it is to see young people who not only love what they do but are proud to be doing it.

Went to a drinks party after that at a great wine bar. The walls were lined with sleek machines that each held about six bottles of wine. At the push of a button, you could fill a glass and the bottle would automatically be resealed and potentially stay fresh for up to three weeks. Machines like these have been around for a while, but these were the nicest and most sophisticated I'd seen. How tempting to put one in the new house. The cast and producers brought out a cake in honor of Felicity's birthday. They sang her praises as well as that song. She is beloved by all of them, and rightly so. She was touched and slightly embarrassed, which made her even more attractive.

August 11

Home by one p.m. from Bristol. Ate pasta with the beans and lentils I had made a few days before. Was famished. Cleaned the large number of onions we had picked at Garsons farm. They were caked with mud, so it took a while. We had picked three large yellow onions and about fifteen red. Unlike those you buy in a shop, these were all different shapes and sizes, their colors and perfume intense. The yellow onions had thick amber skins and white and green flesh that brought tears to my eyes after the first slice. The red onions were the deepest, darkest purple, and after I peeled off the tough outer layer and cleaned them, they seemed to glow from within. I arranged them in a pile on the counter and couldn't stop looking at them, wishing I had the time to paint them. I took photos for future reference.

I decided to use the yellow ones for that night's dinner to accompany two Dutch veal chops, bought on the previous trip to Garsons. Here's what I did, and it was pretty good:

- Sauté the onions with a little olive oil, a smashed garlic clove, white wine, and a little sugar and let them cook down slowly. Transfer to a bowl and set aside. Sear the chops in a little butter and oil for a few minutes on either side, then return the onions to the pan. Add a bay leaf, a sprig of thyme, a bit of rosemary, some chicken stock, and more wine. Turn down the heat, cover it, and let it cook for about 10 minutes.

I made use of some of the red onions for the next night's dinner as follows:

SERVES 2

3 large red onions, thinly sliced, then roughly chopped
8 small anchovies, rinsed and finely chopped
Extra-virgin olive oil
Butter
6 salted, dried capers, roughly chopped
Chicken or vegetable stock
9 ounces spaghetti
Breadcrumbs and chopped parsley, for serving

- In a large pan over medium heat, cook the onions and anchovies in a glug of olive oil and a knob of butter until soft, without letting them brown. Add the capers. Add a couple of ladlefuls (about 2 cups) chicken or vegetable stock and cook for 5 to 10 minutes.
- Meanwhile, boil the spaghetti until al dente. Strain the pasta, reserving a bit of pasta water.
- Add the pasta and a splash of pasta water to the mixture in the pan. Add a bit more butter and olive oil and toss together.
- Serve in a bowl.
- Sprinkle with a handful of breadcrumbs and chopped parsley.

August 12

Felicity, Matteo, Millie, and I are off to Umbria for a week. We will be staying in a house that we rented about seven years ago with a lovely pool and an indoor soft play area. The kids are thrilled. I'm on the fence, only because I have traveled so much already this year that part of me just wants to stay home. I also know how hot it gets in Italy at this time of year. And I hate the heat.

After checking in at Heathrow we headed for my favorite part of the flying process, security. The airport was not very crowded and before we knew it, we were unloading our devices, belts, and appropriately portioned and bagged liquids into gray bins to be examined in the examining machine by a very unhappy-looking uniformed examiner.

In the children's rucksacks were water bottles tucked into side pockets designed specifically for water bottles. Before we placed them in the gray bins, I asked Felicity if they were empty, and she told me they indeed were. She is not one to lie. At least about such things.

Barely a moment had passed after my query and Felicity's assured response when a security officer announced that one of the children's water bottles did indeed have some water in it. I apologized profusely and was about to find a receptacle in which to dispose of the water when she asked if I would drink it. Without a moment's hesitation I obliged by taking a big swig under her watchful gaze. It was less than tepid and tasted like a liquid sock, but I smiled nonetheless at her, as if to say, *See, it's not a flammable liquid, nor is it a poison. It's just water.* She thanked me and I placed the water bottle into the gray bin.

After walking through the metal detector, which miraculously did not go off, as they often do for no reason, we waited for our carry-on luggage to complete its journey.

Unfortunately, one of our bags was redirected to the "other belt," a sign that the unhappy examiner had spotted something that made him even unhappier and warranted further inspection. I sighed and headed to the table where the same security officer who had made me drink the fetid water stood and waited for the gray bin holding the object in question to finish its course. When it had, she grabbed it, placed it on the table between us, and from it plucked the same water bottle I had sipped from only moments before. She then asked the question we all know too well by now: "Is this yours, sir?"

"Yes, it is."

"Do you know this water bottle has water in it?"

"Yes, I do. I just drank from it."

"You can't take it on the plane."

"Why?"

"It's too much liquid to bring on the plane."

"Oh, I thought . . . sorry . . . I thought you just wanted to see me drink it and then you'd know that—"

"You'll have to finish the water, sir."

"Sorry?"

"You'll have to finish the water, sir, or we'll have to confiscate the bottle."

"Well, just . . . I'll just dump it out."

"You can't do that, sir."

"Why?"

"That's not allowed, sir."

"But it's just water. You just saw me—"

"Do you want to finish the water, sir?"

"No. No, I don't want to finish the water. It's disgusting. I just tasted it. It's been in there for . . . It's gross."

"So, you're happy for me to confiscate the bottle then?"

"No. I'm not happy for you to do that." It was a really nice Yeti water bottle, and I was determined not to relinquish it. I pleaded. "Let me . . . Can I . . . can't I just dump out the water?"

"Sorry, sir—"

At this point Felicity arrives and asks what's going on. I explain. She says, "Can't we just dump it out?"

"No, madam. That's against the rules. You either have to drink it or I'll have to confiscate the bottle."

Felicity is also taken aback. "But that's absurd."

A pause. A vague standoff. The security officer is clearly frustrated. (Well, there's irony.) She says, "I'll be right back."

She leaves.

She walks very slowly.

Felicity and I talk.

Probably about Kafka.

The security officer returns with a supervisor, who says, "Sorry, sir, you're going to have to drink the water, or we will have to take the bottle."

"I don't want to drink the water. I already drank the water and it's disgusting."

"Then we'll have to—"

Felicity grabs the bottle and says, "I'll drink it."

She takes off the top and drinks it. She shows the security officer and her supervisor that the water bottle is now empty.

They thank her. She returns to the children, who are standing a few feet away. I angrily begin to pack up my bag and the specious water bottle. Then the security officer asks me in a tiny, sweet voice, "I am racking my brain, but I can't think of the movie that I just love you in!"

My jaw has turned to stone. I almost crack a tooth, I am clenching it so hard. I can't look at her. I am shaking with anger. I mutter, "I've been in a lot of movies."

"I know, but what one—"

"PROBABLY *THE DEVIL WEARS PRADA*!"

She squeals like a schoolgirl, "Ohhhhhh! Yes! That's it! That's the one! I just love you . . ."

I am already walking away so I don't get arrested for doing something that you're not supposed to do to another person.

An ironic postscript: After we boarded the plane Felicity told me that the other water bottle was filled to the brim with water but for some reason wasn't caught by the machines or the liquid-obsessed security officer. Thank God, or Felicity would have spent the entire flight in the loo.

After we landed and I shoved all the suitcases into a car that was meant to be a seven-seater but ended up being only a five-seater, in ninety-five-degree heat, we headed out of Perugia airport toward Città della Pieve to have some lunch.

Città della Pieve is a gorgeous hilltop town that has a vibrant nightlife because unlike many small Italian towns, it has a lot of younger people. The annual Palio was in full swing, an age-old event where three "houses" compete in games and cook for one another over a ten-day period. The streets were filled with residents selling their wares and food as usual on a Saturday, but because of the festival many were dressed in medieval garb, and they were joined by musicians, falconers, and the like. My son Nicolo has been working at Quintosapore, the organic farm that Colin, his wife, Livia, and Livia's twin brothers, Alessandro and Nicola, own, and the latter two have worked their fingers to the bone to create it. It's Nico's second consecutive summer at the farm. Today, he was wearing one of those medieval woolen cassocks and selling potatoes from the farm cooked on an OFYR (a wide cast-iron ring with a fire in the center of it), in the sweltering heat. He's been at the farm for almost a month, picking and sorting vegetables for long hours in the hottest summer on record but having a wonderful time with Colin and Livia's two sons, whom he has known for a decade now.

Moments later we met our friends Danny and Monique, who were joining us for the week, and we all had a lovely lunch in town. Afterward, we drove to the house, unpacked, and opened some wine while the kids played in the soft play area off the living room. The latter space being the real reason we rented the house.

I am becoming obsessed with the allium in all its varieties. Here in Umbria, I bought Tropea onions, which were readily available in the bargain grocery store. I sautéed them in oil, white wine, and a bit of butter. We had them for lunch. I incorporated some of the cooked onions with potatoes into a couple of frittatas. (The rest I saved for the next day and heaped onto *carta di musica*, a crisp flatbread from Sardegna also known as *pane carasau*.) Along with a caprese salad, fresh sheep ricotta, and a green salad, they were a hit. It didn't hurt that we rained some black truffle all over the frittatas.

However, the recent and rather rare allium in which we are now indulging is known as *aglione* and is indigenous to Umbria and its environs. (In Italian, *aglio* is "garlic," so *aglione* basically means "big garlic.") *Aglione* resembles a very large clove of garlic, but the skin is more uniform in color (white with a light brown inside), and it has anywhere between two and six cloves and almost no smell. At Quintosapore, they have planted an entire field of *aglione*, and after we visited one night, they gifted us a hefty amount to take home.

Raw *aglione*, as I said, has almost no smell. However, once cut and cooked, it releases a fragrance somewhere between garlic and onion. When minced, sautéed very gently to the point of emulsification, and cooked with puréed tomatoes, it creates a wonderful and singular-tasting sauce. The only other ingredients added are pecorino Romano, salt, and on occasion pepperoncini.

It is traditionally served with pici, a thick, quite heavy, eggless, spaghetti-like pasta. In Umbria pici is known as umbricelli. The reason for this is that "pici" is the Tuscan name for this type of pasta, and God forbid an Umbrian should use a Tuscan name for anything, especially pasta. And vice versa. When it comes to certain things, the mindset of the medieval city-state is still alive and well throughout all of Italy.

August 16

Had a drink and some appetizers (capicola, prosciutto, focaccia) in the little square of the fairy-tale-beautiful town of Solomeo. The brilliant designer Brunello Cucinelli owns it, which is why it's so stunning, and its streets are cleaner than my kitchen, which is saying a lot.

We ate at a nearby restaurant, where I had gnocchi with *ragù d'oca*, meaning "goose ragù." Although it is an age-old recipe, I had never heard of it until our very first episode of *Searching for Italy*, when we filmed a wheat-threshing festival in the Tuscan countryside.

When Italy was in fact a country of city-states controlled by the church and/or royal families, geese (and all good cuts of all meats) were reserved for those in power, like members of the clergy, royalty, or the "seigneurs," the landed gentry who owned the fields and farms on which the tenant farmers worked.

Yet after the harvest, as an act of gratitude for their toil, the seigneurs gifted a certain number of geese to the farmers, on which the farmers would feast for one night. These geese were roasted in the large communal oven. Some would be broken down and incorporated into a tomato sauce and served with pasta as a first course (not unlike a Bolognese) and the others carved up and served on platters with vegetables on the side as a main course.

The sauce I ate at the restaurant in Umbria was superb, and though differently prepared, it triggered memories of my introduction to this recipe the night we filmed.

Those geese were roasted in large rectangular carbon-steel pans in a formidable wood-fired oven, not by chefs but by local townsmen. When they plucked a sizzling bird from the oven and presented me with a piece, I exclaimed that it tasted like Christmas in my mouth.

The sauce, made with ground goose and prepared by the local townswomen, was cooked slowly for hours in an enormous pot. It emitted an all-consuming aroma wafting from a liquid of oranges, reds, and golds that foretold its complexity. When eaten on a piece of rustic Tuscan bread, it became more than the sum of its parts, and those flavors are now imprinted indelibly on my taste buds. That simple meal, and the ceremony that celebrates and safeguards it, is an invaluable gustatory record of the history of that place and those people.

August 17

As we had another five friends coming for the day, Felicity hired a chef to cook for us, which would allow us to just sit and enjoy ourselves. It was a real treat.

The chef, a polite and shy fellow named Ciro, arrived at about eleven a.m. to set up his kit. He brought an electric pizza oven with two compartments, which he placed on top of the stove; a couple of trays, each containing perfectly shaped domes of pizza dough; and all the necessary toppings, stored in Tupperware containers, which he organized in seconds on the kitchen island. By the time I had returned from a quick wine run, he had lit a fire in the grill (the same grill Nico and I had failed to light a few nights before, about which I will forever be irritated), and the coals were on their way to becoming white-hot. Ciro made and served, with perfect timing, having no assistance from anyone whatsoever, about a dozen pizzas, such as:

Margherita

Quattro formaggi (four cheeses)

Focaccia (olive oil and rosemary)

Broccolini and sausage

Cheese, sausage, and truffle

Margherita and truffle

And they were all delicious.

Then, over the now white-hot coals, he grilled a few T-bone cuts of *bistecca alla fiorentina*. (The beef used for *bistecca alla fiorentina* comes from a rare breed of white cow that feeds only on grass and whose meat is some of the tastiest in the world.) Ciro cooked portions of the meat rare and others just a bit more for those who like their meat cooked . . . just a bit more.

Having stood next to the late, great Fabio Picchi, one of the masters of *bistecca alla fiorentina*, I can say that Ciro was very much his equal. I'm sure Fabio would have been happy.

The side dishes were simple as usual but always great: boiled bitter greens dressed with oil and lemon, and a mixed green salad with vinaigrette.

And we had wine. Both hues.

Full disclosure:

The hard part about writing this book is that my taste buds have a very strong memory and if the food I am writing about at any given time was food I liked, they are triggered, and I must run to the kitchen to eat. I'd better finish this book soon or I'll end up paying frequent visits to a very fortunate tailor.

August 19

Flew home with no trouble at all and settled in quickly. Although our stay in Umbria was truly wonderful, I am happy to be home. Each day in Umbria was hotter than the one before, and as I've mentioned, I cannot bear the heat. I love the *sun* but not the *heat*. The ideal solar experience for me comes at the end of a day on the slopes as I sip an après-ski cocktail in the winter sun. (What a snooty sentence that is.)

August 22

Emily, John, and their girls have arrived, which had our kids going wild. For two weeks Matteo and Millie asked us hourly when their cousins were coming, and when they did, all four of them were inseparable. Over the next few days I stayed home as much as possible doing as little as possible and hanging around with Em and John and the kids, which was very satisfying. I ventured out one day to take Matteo to the doctor to have his tonsils and adenoids checked, as he is prone to strep throat and is a "heavy breather," as they say. After a quick peek at both, the doctor told us that he would indeed benefit from having them removed. He said the heavy breathing along with his snoring would cease, the slightly dark circles under his eyes would disappear, and his sense of taste would be improved by the removal of his adenoids. He said that children will often put on a bit of weight after the procedure as they eat more because swallowing is easier, and everything tastes better. After hearing that there is now a basically bloodless method of removing the tonsils, allowing the patient to eat normally that same day, Matteo was happy to agree to the operation and we set a date. Very curious to see if his taste will indeed be improved. I'm tempted to get mine removed as well.

August 25–September 1

The Blunt-Tucci-Krasinski troupe headed to the Cotswolds to stay in the same house we had stayed in a few months before. Monique and Danny were meeting us there. (We cannot take a vacation without them because they just make everyone happier.)

The people:

6 adults

4 children

The provisions:

2 extra-large saucepans (a sixteen-inch saucepan and a fourteen-inch Stanley Pan)

My favorite knife

1 cocktail shaker

2 sets of tongs

Pasta: approximately eight 1-pound packets in assorted shapes

Rice: 1 pound

Risotto rice: 6½ pounds

Olive oil: Two 1-quart bottles of regular, Filippo Berio, and one

5-quart bottle of our favorite extra-virgin that we use every day, Il Cavallino, from Tuscany

1 large box of kosher salt

12 bottles of beer

18 bottles of red wine

18 bottles of white wine

3 bottles of vodka

4 bottles of tequila

3 bottles of scotch

1 bottle of vermouth

3 bottles of gin*

3 cases of San Pellegrino

4½-pound chunk of Parmigiano

A variety of other soft and hard cheeses

3 loaves of bread

6 packages each of salami, prosciutto, and ham

3 bunches of rainbow chard

2 bunches of kale

8 zucchini

---

* We were expecting a large influx of guests throughout the week, hence the number of libations.

4 heads of lettuce

12 potatoes

2 flats of tomatoes, different varieties

3 bunches of basil

2 bunches of parsley

1 bunch of bananas

8 oranges

1 flat of mixed apples, peaches, and pears

1 bag of tangerines

12 lemons

12 limes

2 half gallons of orange juice

4 quarts of milk

3¼ pounds of butter

1 quart of oat milk

1 quart of almond milk

4 heads of garlic

3 *aglioni* (left over from Umbria)

3 black truffles (also left over from Umbria and smuggled in)

6 yellow onions

8 red onions (left over from the Garsons farm picking spree)

3 dozen eggs

2 boxes of very sugary kids' breakfast cereal (because it's a holiday)

2 jars of jam

1 plastic squeeze container of honey

4 packets of chicken breasts

4 packets of chipolata sausages

2¼ pounds of ground beef

Two more adults and one child arrived on Sunday.
By Monday, somehow a trip to the grocery store was necessary.

The first night, Ian Ballantyne, a freelance chef who was never professionally trained but seems to be able to cook anything very, very well, let the kids assemble their own pizzas, which made them ecstatically happy to the point that they would chant his name hourly when we told them he was to return in a couple of nights. It's not every chef who is able to connect with children and effortlessly integrate them into the joys of cooking. Ian did indeed come again a couple of times, making more pizza, miso-glazed eggplant, roasted potato salad, roasted sea bass, and various cuts of veal and dairy-cow beef, which were grilled to perfection.

That week the routine was basically as follows:

In the morning at about nine, we would all exercise with Monique, our friend and trainer, then we'd play a couple of hours of tennis, make a huge lunch (*avec vin*), play more tennis, swim with the kids, and go for a walk in the fields or nap.

Five p.m.: Cocktails.

Then . . .

Bathe the children.

Feed the children.

Place the children in front of a film.

Then, cook.

Here is what we cooked that week for either lunch or dinner:

Tagliatelle all'aglione

Risotto with zucchini and asparagus

Orecchiette with pesto, potatoes, and green beans

Flank steak seared in oil and butter and red wine

Frittatas with mushrooms and black truffle

Smashed burgers with Emily's burger sauce and fries

Green salads

Cucumber salads

Tomato salads (sometimes with thinly sliced red onions)

Emily's kale, lettuce, and cucumber salad

Cannellini beans, red onions, and canned tuna

Green beans with vinaigrette

Pasta bakes (one with leftovers of the wonderful Bolognese Emily made for the kids and one with just plain tomato sauce; Fee and I added béchamel to both)

Orecchiette with sautéed onions, garlic, zucchini, and lots of Parmigiano

In addition to John and Emily, their two girls, Danny, Monique, and the four of us Tuccis, there were friends coming and going the entire week: Jonny Cournoyer, an artist and photographer and John Krasinski's best mate; his wife, Jenn Streicher; and their lovely ten-year-old son, Arrow; David and Georgia Tennant; and Cillian Murphy and his wife, Yvonne McGuinness.

Having finally gotten over my starstruckedness, I was able to chat to Cillian and Yvonne, and they could not have been more interesting, kind, or funny. Yvonne is a multifaceted artist and also someone who more than knows her way around a tennis court. Cillian himself is an excellent table tennis player. He and I played three games, and although I won the first, he won the next two. I will demand a rematch, as I was at a disadvantage because I probably was still a little starstruck. But between us, now that I've gotten to know Yvonne, his star has been eclipsed.

I love holidays like this because I really love cooking for lots of people who appreciate food and are also willing to help. Although I'm happy to "relax" with a book or a sketchpad, at a certain point I *must* get up and move. And when I move, if it doesn't take the form of exercise, I want to move in front of a stove.

Yet I must contradict myself. (Why not? Everyone else contradicts me.) As much as I love cooking with people, I am also more than happy to cook alone. Obviously cooking has a practical purpose but often for me it's just using food for thought.

By this I mean, the task at hand focuses a certain part of my mind, which in turn allows whatever is left to explore other thoughts, ideas, problems, or fears that have been unknowingly awaiting rumination. When I cook alone, I'm free to think about how I might, say, write a certain passage of this book, how I might correct or improve a certain passage, or if I should just stop writing altogether; how I might write a scene for a script I'm working on; how I might address a scene I will act in the next day; or how I rue the way I acted in a scene the day before. I may ponder why I'm obsessed with Chekhov's plays, especially *Uncle Vanya* and *The Cherry Orchard*, where his characters are so unhappy because they all live the way they *think* they should live but not how they *want* to live, and how their ideas of life get in the way of action and truth, which is why his plays are so brilliant and enduring. How my folks are faring in Florida, a place still foreign to them, so far away, and how sad and guilty that makes me feel, how each of my sisters is getting by on separate coasts in the confused country that is today's America, how the older kids are doing and how I only want them to be happy, how I am too far along in years to ever grow old with the lanky, beautiful, brilliant woman I love and help look after her when *she* grows old, what it will be like when I am standing at our kitchen stove and Matteo no longer asks me to make him lunch but does so on his own for what I know will be his very tall self, or the day when Millie will round the corner of the island on which the stove sits and her deep brown eyes will no longer gaze upward at mine but will be on the same plane, and in a new and different voice she will ask me what we're having for dinner.

September 4

Matteo and Millie's first day of school. Millie is in her second year and Matteo has moved up into the "eights." He no longer wears a uniform and will have a different teacher in a different classroom for each subject. It's a big transition. When they came home, I expected a lot of talk about new teachers, subjects, fellow students, and so on, but they were as taciturn as most kids of any age are about school after the first day or almost any day.

"How was school?"

"Good."

Silence.

I assume it went well.

September 5

Felicity worked from home in her office navigating Zoom calls, phone calls, and so on. I was in my office writing this book.

After the kids came home from school, we took them for a stroll in the park. Matteo tried to catch fish in his "fish trap," to no avail, and Fee and Millie picked the quickly fading blackberries. I fluttered between both unsuccessful activities. It was hot, and according to the weather report it will remain so for the next week or more. Yet another visceral testament to global warming.

Arriving home, the kids showered while I made a martini and Fee cooked hamburgers for them with defrosted mince from the farmers' market. Unfortunately, we had to discard it as it tasted too "beefy." It's not that it was "off," it's just that its flavor was so strong that basically, it eclipsed itself. (This is the same beef my mother used for the meatballs and that I insisted was great and that she did not care for because it was too beefy. Perhaps she was right. Damn it! She's not. The fellow sells great mince. I blame that certain cow.) Luckily there was other mince.

Felicity cooked that up in the form of hamburgers, which, thankfully, the kids ate, and then we watched a few Pixar shorts, which were brilliantly funny. (Why don't they write stuff like that for live action? I'd sign up.)

After the children were asleep, Felicity, being slightly under the weather, excused herself to bed. Since I had not eaten since midafternoon (a quick repast of stuffed grape leaves, hummus, crackers, and *taramasalata*), I sautéed some onion; added leftover puréed tomato sauce, leftover peas, a dot of butter, grated Parmigiano, a splash of white wine, a few torn basil leaves, and a drizzle of EVOO; and cooked it in a saucepan for about fifteen minutes. I boiled some pasta (tubetti), tossed it all together, ate two bowls of the stuff accompanied by a glass of red wine, and then wrote about it. Which is what you just read. And then I went to bed.

Ode to a Dirty Bird

A free-form recipe-poem à la e. e. cummings

I made pigeon breast the other night.

It was good.

like this:

pigeon breasts

5

In a marinade

of:

red wine
sherry vinegar
juniper berries
black pepper

olive oil
soy sauce
red onion
fresh thyme
fresh rosemary

marinate

1 hour.

at end of hour

a cast-iron pan

made **hot**

pl^{u}ck
from marinade
the pigeon b.

pat
dry

butter - knob

olive oil: drizzllllle

in

that **hot** pan.

sear

PIGEON BREASTS

Quickly!!
then . . .

breasts on _______platter___________

there's the marinade and there's the pan . . .
(*pour it in!*}

reduce

pour
over
p. breasts.

Serve

with/con/avec/mit/med/com

polenta
or

mashed potato

or

risotto (saffron?)

and . . . . . bitter, bitter, bitter, bitter greens.

eat. EAT!

&
drink

{**red wine!**) ++++.

oh, yum. Oh, yum, oh, oh, and oh,,,,,, ...

September 6

Did a Q and A with Kate Mosse, the talented British author, not the model, to raise money for the Women's Prize for Fiction at the Barbican. She and Felicity are both on the board. Due to the SAG strike, I had to somehow talk about my forty-two-year-long career in show business without mentioning any film or television show I've ever been a part of because that would be a form of publicity, which is not allowed during a strike. So basically, we discussed acting and filmmaking in general terms and food in detail. Kate was brilliant as usual and made it so easy for me. I guess I passed muster, because my SAG membership has not been revoked. It was so heartening to see that so much of the audience were people in their twenties and thirties who were there to support such a worthy cause. There is hope for books.

September 7

Harry S. came for dinner. He cycled to our house after working out in Mayfair. We had not seen him for a long time. It was just the three of us. He's done with his tour and taking a much-deserved break. As he is a pescatarian I made a leek and zucchini risotto with a quick veg stock I cooked up, followed by cod *alla livornese*, which I can't seem to get enough of these days. Felicity made a carrot salad. We drank tequila and wine and Harry brought one of the best single-malt scotches I've ever tasted. We talked a lot about books and love. Harry is a voracious reader. He's reading Rilke now. He's a thoughtful and kind fellow. Not Rilke. Harry. I never knew Rilke.

September 8

Felicity and I should have been eating lunch on the shores of Lake Como today, but the flight was canceled yesterday due to an airline workers' strike in Italy. Not unlike the French, Italians are so good at striking that they could make it a profession. But then how would they rally against any inequities? (Not dissimilar to the guy who said he was against protesting but didn't know how to express it.) Anyway, instead of heading to Como we took a train to Bristol to see the last day of the *Rivals* shoot and go to the wrap party. We will go to Como tomorrow. Felicity will stay for only two nights, and I will stay for another couple of days to film content for San Pellegrino.

Had oysters, serrano ham, focaccia, and Vesper martinis at Rick's again in Bristol. Loveliest staff and proper bartenders. Great place. Party at a nearby hotel was fun, but I somehow missed the food that was being dished out. Jilly Cooper was there and as charming as ever, as was her assistant Amanda. Felicity was so happy and looked beautiful in a blue-and-white-striped Lee Mathews dress. Went to bed too late in our shitty hotel.

September 9

Had a big, pretty good breakfast in that shitty hotel. Eggs, croissant, mushrooms, hash browns, orange juice. Lots of fat and grease. Headed to train station. Train to Paddington delayed.

Arrived an hour late into Paddington station. Made it to Heathrow from Paddington via the Heathrow Express, which was running on schedule, but our flight was delayed (as usual), so it didn't matter.

Why don't airlines just tell their customers that all their flights are leaving an hour later than they really are? Then the airline will have a better chance of being on time. Like setting your watch ten minutes ahead so you're not late. It helps. (Not for me but for some people.) It's a stupid idea, I know, but someone must address the fact that as airline prices increase, the quality of service and on-time performance decreases.

The irony is that after you finally board the delayed flight, the attendants instantly start haranguing everyone to store their luggage and take their seats as quickly as possible so the plane can take off. They act as if *we* were the ones who caused the delay.

Then once everyone has frantically shoved their luggage into the overhead bins and squeezed themselves into their seats (which, along with the legroom between them, shrink every year), and every man, woman, and child is soaked with sweat from the anxiety the flight attendants have triggered, the plane will inevitably sit on the tarmac for a while before it begrudgingly pulls away from the gate and then just taxis around on some sort of unneeded and unwanted sightseeing tour of the airport for a while before it finally takes the f— off, and people either miss connecting flights or get to their hotels and homes hours after they should have. And to top it all off, the food is dreadful. Maybe if the food were better, we could all endure it. I must write a letter.

I've been thinking a lot recently about planting. Cultivating. Cultivation. We're going to plant a large vegetable and herb garden on our new property as well as a small orchard of fruit trees. The second house that Kate and I lived in together had a small orchard of apple trees, some of which were so old that even the arborist who looked after them had no idea what species they were. (Mind you, the house was built in 1738, which is very old for America.)

In my last home in the US, where Felicity came to live with me, Nico, Isabel, and Camilla (and the one that Willie Geist stole from me), Kate and I planted three apple trees, one for each child, and at the house in Devon it's my intention to plant one for each child again. That means at least five. Not that I plan on having more children, I just mean we will probably plant more than five trees.

Why does gardening become a common pastime when people grow older? Is it because after years of dealing with humans it's just easier to spend time with something that needs attention, gives sustenance, and enhances your world but doesn't talk back? Possibly for some of us. And for others, maybe, when age creeps its way in, we innately feel the need to cultivate and encourage life, especially if that life is perennial, because ours, very much, is not.

September 10

Lake Como.

Got to the beautiful Mandarin Hotel and sat down to dinner at nine thirty p.m., famished. Had martinis and a Japanese meal, which was lovely. Slept.

I love Lake Como. I've only been a few times, but it might be the place in Italy I am most drawn to. Its beauty is staggering, and I find solace in the proud constancy of the Alps. The sight of those snow-covered mountains gives me great joy, as I adore winter. At the first sight of falling snow, I become childishly gleeful, so for me to be able to see snow, even from a distance, all year round is a great gift.

For millennia the Alps have defined that region of the world geographically and aesthetically. Humankind has revered them, cursed them, admired them, scaled them, sliced into them, bored through them, built upon them, hiked them, lived on them, skied down them, cultivated them, painted them, photographed them, filmed them, argued over them, fought brutal battles on and among them, "conquered" them, and perished because of them. And yet, unmoved by it all, there they stand, absolute, elegantly dressed in white.

September 11

Did yoga with Monique via Zoom in a room overlooking the lake. Idyllic. Hired a boat to take us to Bellagio, where we had a wonderful meal at Bilacus. Amazing service, delicious food (grilled octopus and squid with cream of peas, tagliatelle with shrimp, and grilled whole fish with olive oil and lemon). The wine cellar, curated by Aurelio Gandola, was an oenophile's dream. (What exactly we drank I couldn't tell you, but I remember being just fine with it.) The place was filled with a mix of locals, tourists, families. Discreet, low-key, casually elegant. A perfect Italian restaurant. Lake Como is where Felicity and I met, during her sister Emily's wedding. We chatted a lot during that two-day fête and began dating when I visited London soon after. My God, is she lucky.

Dinner at hotel again. Worked for San Pellegrino the next two days, then flew home Tuesday night.

September 13

Tired after a workout and meeting with the project commissioner of National Geographic and BBC Studios for the Italian series. Probably feeling lousy because I ate poorly once work began on Monday. Unpacked from trip but will only have to pack again in two days' time as I must go to NYC to do press and an event for the cookware launch. I'm happy about the cookware but wish that Felicity were going with me, and I hate leaving the kids. But then I will be home for a bit. Edward Berger is coming for dinner and has informed me that he eats everything. Thank God. Kind of want to make veal Milanese.

We are planning a party. Not sure why, but Fee and I both had the same thought when our trip to Marrakech for a friend's birthday party next weekend was canceled. We are using the excuse that our eleventh wedding anniversary is on the twenty-ninth, and that's a good enough excuse for us. How is it possible that eleven years have passed? It seems like twenty-five. For Felicity, I mean. For me, but a moment.

We are inviting seventy people.

I hope we have room.

Invites going out today.

Part of me hopes that not everyone can make it.

But there is an actors' strike, which means most film and television production has shut down, here and in the US.

And many of the people we invited are in show business.
Well . . .
I guess it will be quite a night.
What's worse than no one showing up to a party?
Everyone showing up.

Edward came for dinner. What a nice, smart fellow. Please, let him cast me in everything he does. Cannot wait to see *Conclave*. I made risotto with a bit of saffron and mushrooms and rabbit legs.

Rabbit Legs

- Marinate rabbit legs in olive oil, garlic, red onion, salt, a splash of sherry vinegar, thyme, rosemary, bay leaf, and peppercorns for at least an hour, or longer if you wish.
- Make a fresh tomato sauce with onion, carrot, celery, garlic, fresh pomodorini, basil, salt, and a little white wine. Cook for about 15 minutes.
- Heat a large oven-safe saucepan (one that can fit in your oven) over medium-high heat and drizzle in some olive oil.
- Remove the rabbit legs from the marinade and pat dry. Sear the rabbit in the pan to color it slightly.
- Preheat the oven to 435°F.
- Strain the marinade. Add it to the pan with the tomato sauce and white wine and chicken stock to cover. Bring to a boil, then reduce

the heat to a simmer and cover. Let it cook for about 20 minutes, turning once, basting on occasion.

- Place the covered pan into the oven for another 20 minutes, basting a couple of times.
- Serve with mashed potatoes, polenta, or risotto, and something green.

September 14

After a workout, I had a fitting for press in NYC to launch the cookware line. I like fittings because, as I've expressed, I like clothes. My father's maternal uncles owned a haberdashery in Peekskill, New York, where I was born, called Pisani Brothers. I remember going there as a young boy a few times and thinking the racks of perfectly organized jackets, suits, shirts, and ties were so beautiful. This was in the 1960s, when most men still dressed in suits and ties every day. I remember the rich earthy palette of the clothing, all deep greens, grays, and dark blues. If I squinted my eyes and looked down the length of the shop, I could see hints of ochre from the camel-hair blazers pop here and there, along with the inevitable Prince of Wales light gray plaid punctuated with its ubiquitous subtle deep-red lines. I loved the feel of all the fabrics but especially the different weights of wool, to which I continue to be drawn to this day. I still buy off-white woolen tennis socks like those I wore as a kid, all my winter thermal wear is merino wool, and I have quite a few wool blazers. Wool is one of the reasons I love autumn and winter so much. And vice versa I guess.

After the fitting, I had lunch with Nico at Quo Vadis. He chose it because a friend from culinary school is working there now. I was thrilled because I love the place and Chef Jeremy Lee is a friend of ours. We featured Quo Vadis on *Searching for Italy* because it was opened by an Italian almost a century ago. He was a chef and restaurateur who took classic Italian dishes and Frenchified them, because basically French restaurants were the only kind of restaurant there was in London. British restaurants didn't really exist, except for pubs, and Italian restaurants were considered lower-class. Jeremy has made Quo Vadis an extraordinary restaurant that serves up superb, elegant versions of British classics such as savory pies, salsify, smoked-eel sandwiches, pan-fried skate with homemade tartar sauce, and so on.

Nico and I had an Italian beer, Menabrea (from Lombardy), at the small club upstairs, as we booked late and they didn't have a table for about forty-five minutes. It was a hot day, and the beer was just what a body needed after a very sticky trip on a very crowded tube.

When our table was ready our waiter, Antonio from Portugal, suggested an albariño, and we took his advice. We had missed out on the savory pies but there was plenty of great stuff left. Here is what we ordered, followed by my reactions:

Thick toasted bread with beetroot purée, figs, goat cheese curd, and honey: Good God.

Smoked eel sandwich (lightly smoked eel with a delicate horseradish mayo on grilled buttered bread): Literally one of the best things I have ever eaten.

Celeriac and fennel salad with a light vinaigrette: Crunchy, fresh, and perfectly cut the richness of the eel.

Small skate wing dusted with flour, panfried in butter, and served with a homemade tartar sauce: So simple. So clean. The warm fish, coupled with a dollop of the almost cool, silken tartar sauce (with just the right amount of zazz from the capers and pickles), made me so happy that I had just eaten it and sad that I've never made it.

We saw Jeremy before we left and heaped endless praise upon his six-foot-three-inch frame, to which he responded with his usual self-deprecatory mutterings.

Had dinner at one of Felicity's colleagues' incredibly beautiful house. I could eat very little, not only because I'd had a big lunch but because there was nothing soft or not spicy being served. But I had been well sated prior and there was lovely bread and wine on the table.

September 15

I had lunch with my cousin Jeff and his wife, Sara, at the River Café. They were in town from Seattle briefly and I had not seen them in a few years. We talked about family, of course, and how we still both love the Tucci family *timpano* that was made every Christmas (and featured in the film *Big Night*) and the fact that Jeff and Sara are devoted to making it every year in their house outside of Seattle. We spent so many Christmases together when we were young. Jeff's parents, Dora and Bob (my aunt and uncle who had those cool cars I mentioned earlier), were a big part of our lives when my sisters and I were growing up, as they lived on the same road as we did for many years. I stayed with them for the summer after my sophomore year at college in their stunning New York City apartment overlooking the East River. On my days off from working as a bartender, my aunt Dora and I would go to museums together, or wander the streets of Manhattan and browse Bloomingdale's or Bergdorf's, as she loved clothing and was always impeccably dressed. Like my parents, she was an inspiration for me when it came to things sartorial. She would often treat me to lunch someplace that was the opposite of the cheap diners where I normally found sustenance. We would also go to her favorite Italian food shops and return to the apartment with the spoils, and I would help her with the meal. She was a wonderful cook who, because she was my father's sister, prepared many of the dishes that were made in my home. I loved spending time with her, and though she was very different from my mother (Aunt

Dora never stopped talking and my mother does not waste words), I found the same comfort and warmth that I did when being with my mom. I also loved that she used excessive amounts of salt in just about everything she made. For all those reasons she was like a second mother to me. She passed away over a decade ago and I miss her every day. Jeff, Sara, and I ate a huge amount of the River Café's consistently delicious food and continued to chat well into the afternoon. They are two people in their late sixties who love to cook, eat, appreciate wine, and yet still remain fit. It can be done, and they are doing it. The next day they were on their way to the Cotswolds for a two-week-long hike. Impressive.

Had dinner at home that night with Felicity and the kids. We made casarecce with a fresh tomato sauce and scallops. The kids ate pasta pesto, then we watched a bit of *The Little Mermaid.*

September 16

Lottie and I flew to NYC for the cookware launch, about which I was at once excited and horrified (meaning nervous). Had a croissant in the airport lounge. Because the flight was going to be a long one due to a storm that needed to be circumvented, I decided to eat the food on the plane. I ordered the salmon. But like a rock star with a fluctuating identity, what arrived was a piece of fish *formerly known as salmon*. I dared two bites of what seemed like softened fiberglass and gave up. I nibbled at a very white roll and watched a couple of movies.

After an endless ride from JFK to Manhattan, we checked into the Whitby Hotel, which is part of the Firmdale group. I love staying in their hotels because there's a consistency of eccentric, cozy design; they are spotlessly clean and beautifully appointed; and the staff is kind. I first stayed in one, the Covent Garden Hotel in London, over twenty years ago with Kate while promoting *Big Night*. We had the loveliest time together that trip, and it was the first time I'd ever seen an honesty bar, which is a staple in all Firmdale hotels.

Another property of theirs, the Charlotte Street Hotel, is where I stayed while filming *Captain America* and where Felicity and I first spent time together, as they say. It was in the Charlotte Street (after a drink at Ronnie Scott's, where I told Emily that Felicity and I were dating and Felicity got miffed because she wanted to tell Emily herself but I said I had the right to spill the beans because Emily was my friend first) that Chris Evans, Hayley Atwell, Dominic Cooper, Emily and Susannah Blunt, Felicity, and I played running charades in the honesty bar until two a.m., to the irritation of the staff. I've been lucky to stay in many lovely hotels over the years as I've traveled for work. I have also been *unlucky* to stay in a lot of *unlovely* hotels over the years, some of them independently owned, others part of a larger brand. When we make our way through Italy filming *Where the F . . . Is Italy, Stan?*, because of the budget, number of people, and distance to and from locations, we often stay in those *unlovely* hotels. Yes, there have been times when we've been able to ensconce ourselves in a well-appointed place, but normally for only a night or two as the stories we are filming require us to pick up and move, sometimes up to three or four times in a week. Unfortunately, traveling endlessly through Italy has taught me that quite often, "five-star hotel" does not mean what we think it means. Italian hoteliers must count stars differently than they do other objects, because when it comes to hotel stars the number *five* is equal to the number *one*. My advice is that the next time you travel to the Italian peninsula, be on the lookout for a twenty-five-star hotel and you're certain to have a five-star experience.

Had dinner at Nobu in NYC. Very good as usual. Those battered rock shrimp. Just kill me.

September 17

Woke up too early and ordered breakfast. Steel-cut oats and a bagel with smoked salmon and cream cheese. Went to the gym about an hour later. Arrived at the Williams Sonoma store at Columbus Circle and saw the amazing display of the cookware line, did some social media filming, and signed about five hundred books for about five hundred people who had queued up for a long time. It was a bit overwhelming because they were all so excited to meet me. I am better at dealing with it now than a few years ago. I used to be extremely embarrassed. However, I soon learned that my embarrassment was not conducive to making anyone feel comfortable, particularly those who had waited far too long for a signature, so I made a conscious choice to "let it go." My embarrassment is born of an innate guilt at being successful, even though success is what I have always sought. I believe most of my humility has remained intact. Although you may have to ask my wife and children about that. Actually, don't. I signed for three hours straight, then went back to the hotel and rested.

In the evening we had martinis at the hotel, then walked to the Polo Bar, where we had some great old-fashioned American chophouse-like food—Reuben sandwiches, burgers, Caesar salads, and the like. I love all that stuff.

September 18

This morning, after a rushed workout because I couldn't drag myself out of the extremely comfortable bed, I did two cooking segments on the *Today* show and a sit-down interview to promote the cookware. The hosts are so nice and always make you feel at ease. But the pace of the cooking segments is so fast that no cooking is actually done. Everything is pre-prepared, in this case by a wonderful young chef named Katie and her team, and all you do is basically stand in front of the mobile cooking unit and point to the dish in its various stages as you explain the recipe. I don't know why it must be that rushed, but having done it many times, I am used to it now.

We ate lunch at a expensive but delicious Japanese place on the Upper East Side. It was the only place we could find that would take five people, as most good restaurants were booked due to the number of diplomats that are in town for the UN summit. In fact, today the traffic was especially terrible because Biden and Zelensky (my hero) are both in town. If someone like Zelensky is the reason for gridlock, that's fine with me, but it proves once again that the "grid" structure of New York City's streets was not made for a multitude of motor vehicles, because it "locks." Oh, for a London roundabout.

After lunch I headed uptown to my oncologist, Dr. Bakst, who kindly made time to see me. I had blood drawn that would be tested for any vestiges of the small squamous cell cancer that might be lurking in my system. Only this cancer, caused by the HPV virus, can be detected through a blood test, which is even more exacting in its results than any scan. I will get the result in ten days.*

Dr. Bakst also showed me some research he's been doing on oral bacteria and diet as they relate to head and neck cancers and cancer in general. He is discovering that certain bacterial imbalances can promote and foster cancer development. By finding which bacteria are either overabundant or lacking in a patient's mouth, doctors may be able to prescribe supplements or recommend foods and simple ways (proper brushing, fluoride, alkalizing the mouth and/or gut) to bring the body and its metabolism back into balance, therefore halting the disease before it has a chance to take root or helping the healing process if it has already presented itself. Dr. Bakst and I had spoken about this when I was ill because I am fascinated by cancer and its causes, and he was kind enough to indulge me. We talked about diet and how crucial it is to cancer prevention and treatment, and this research makes the connection even more apparent. I asked him why cancer is more prevalent now than years ago. Is it because we test more, or do we just know more about it? He said that first, people are living longer, and the longer you live, the more likely you are to get cancer. But he also said that there is a concerning spike in cancer cases in people under the age of fifty and that this is likely due to diet and lifestyle. It makes sense. We become what we eat. Eat unhealthily, become unhealthy. Of course, there are exceptions, but for the most part it's true.

* * *

* The results of my scan and blood test were both negative. This means I have hit the crucial five-year mark with NED (no evidence of disease). After five years it is highly unlikely that the cancer will return. So that's good.

Flew to Florida with Lottie to visit my folks. Was feeling a bit under the weather with a cold and aching joints. Lottie felt off as well but not as poorly as I did.

My folks kindly picked us up at eleven p.m. When we got back to the condo, we ate pasta with sautéed zucchini and onions that my mother had prepared for us. It was delicious of course, and much appreciated, as the food on the plane was not even food. Although what I ate in the lounge wasn't terrible. They had "Italian wedding soup," which is chicken broth, escarole, and a small pasta similar to couscous, followed by grilled vegetable wraps. Not so bad in comparison to the gunk and gurry usually served to most travelers.

September 19

This morning we went to the beach for a couple of hours, then came home and ate lunch, which consisted of tabouli my mother had made the day before, cannellini beans (with tuna, tomato, red onion, and basil), chicken livers with peppers and onions, escarole and beans, bread, and wine. If you're looking for a healthy meal, you just read what one is.

My father is doing much better than when I last saw him. He is still moving slowly, mostly due to his knee, but his spirits and energy are very good, and he is very engaged and chatty, as is my ageless mother.

In the evening we made saffron *risotto con funghi*, with the new cookware I had sent them. Lottie filmed it all so we could get my mother's assessment, critique, thoughts, musings, suggestions, and so on about the pans. (You can view this on Instagram.) All in all, her reviews were positive. Thank God. There were complaints, however, about food getting caught where the handles connect to the exterior of the pan and how it seemed difficult to clean the brushed stainless-steel surface. She wasn't wrong, but a little elbow grease and Bob's your uncle, as they say. Then we ate the risotto, which we critiqued no end until we finished it. Then we had a salad.

September 20

We visited the Williams Sonoma store in a mall about forty minutes away. It was a very high-end shopping mecca that covered acres and acres of some of the flattest land in America.

The landscape and climate of Florida are not for me, and I struggle with them, along with the "architecture," whenever I'm there. It makes me wonder when we stopped caring about what things look like. When did thoughtful design cease to matter? Was there one day when the majority of people who design and build things all got together and just said, *Fuck it. It doesn't matter anymore. Who cares? Walls, a roof, a door, windows (maybe), that's all it needs. I mean really, just . . . fuck it. Here's a building, just put stuff inside it and sell it. That's all people really care about anyway.*

If you build it, they will come.

No matter what it looks like.

And they were right.

Anyway, the people at the Williams Sonoma shop were lovely and very happy we stopped by, and the display looked great. The line has been selling like hotcakes and we are all thrilled. (I have never eaten a hotcake, nor have I ever seen anyone selling them. Maybe because they sell them so fast that they are gone before I get there.)

Driving home, Lottie and I discovered that our flight had been canceled. No reason given. Gee, what a shock. (I am so tempted to name the airline, but I won't.) In fact, we have started to use a wonderful travel agent because there are so many cancellations by the airlines and changes in our schedules that Lottie and Felicity and our children's nanny and assistant, Nela, could not manage it without it taking up the better part of a day. I never attempted to deal with it.

After a lunch of leftovers and risotto cakes, Lottie made her way to Orlando (a two-and-a-half-hour drive that became a three-and-a-half-hour drive due to traffic) to get a direct flight home, which was delayed by an hour or more. I was feeling unwell and had been sweating through the night, so I took to my bed with an apple and a good book.

In the evening my parents and I ate chicken wings, steak *oreganato*, baked potatoes, and leftover escarole and beans. I left soon afterward, having been moved to a direct flight on another airline from Tampa (an hour away), which ended up leaving two and a half hours late, meaning one a.m. I had arrived at the airport at nine p.m.

September 22–27

I arrived home at two thirty p.m. having slept on the plane, thanks to pharmaceuticals. Felicity looked at me when I entered and from a distance said, "I bought you a Covid test."

"Oh," I said. "Do you think I should—"

"Yes," she said.

So, I did.

And it was positive.

And I was furious.

I had been away for a week and all I wanted was to hug and kiss my wife and kids, and neither of those things was going to happen for a while. I was already cranky, and the news added a dose of petulance to my emotional mix. I have traveled endlessly around the world for the last three years, been tested countless times, felt unwell many times, but never tested positive, and yet *this* is the *one time* I test positive?!? *This* trip, to visit my aging parents so I can spend some quality time with them in the winter of their years! Really!?!

Felicity calmed me down as usual.

We called my parents and alerted them. Two days later we got a call that my father was in the hospital with Covid and pneumonia in one lung. They put him on intravenous antibiotics. By the next day he was a bit better, but then they removed the IV and he was told that the pneumonia was Covid induced and that the antibiotics would not work. That was confusing. But they gave him remdesivir to treat the virus.

I am very nervous about his condition, especially since I am undoubtedly the one who gave him the virus.

The hardest thing about aging is how quickly it happens and how slowly it occurs. I know that this has been said by someone before, but aging is the hands of a clock. We never see them move, but they do. You look away for what seems like just a moment and the next time you look back, it's much later than you thought.

I have been unable to taste anything for a few days now due to Covid. This is disconcerting of course for anyone, but for me, having my taste and smell corrupted for a long time after my cancer treatments and having slowly regained them over the past five years, to the point where they are more acute than ever, this turn of events is worrisome to say the least. In most Covid cases one's taste and smell will return within two weeks after testing negative for the virus, yet in some cases their absence can linger for months, and sometimes, although rarely, the loss can be long-term. Of course, the latter is my greatest fear. If I am unable to taste, not only will I find life unbearable, but I will be unable to carry out what has now become a crucial part of my work, namely, *tasting*. Within a couple of months, we're scheduled to film more episodes of the yet unnamed *Stan Once Again Goes to Italy Show*, and if my sense of taste and smell have disappeared or are even dulled, it will be impossible for me to do so. Although I pride myself on my acting ability, I could never in good conscience "fake taste" my way through the Italian peninsula, or any other country for that matter. I can only hope that both taste and smell return before too long or I will have to put an end to my filmed gustatory treks. This would make me sad because I love doing the show and I know how happy it makes people. It is also not a small part of my income. Hmm . . .

Well, maybe I *could* fake it.

September 28

I tested myself yet again this morning (I tested five times yesterday), and there is still the faintest of red lines that suggests there is a hint of the virus remaining. The positive line has faded more and more with each test, which is heartening but also annoying. Felicity thinks I'm mad to keep testing, but I am now addicted to it. I just want it to be over and done with.

September 29

I have tested negative. My sense of taste and smell are returning, albeit slowly. The last time this happened (just before the first lockdown I thought I had a flu for about a day and a half and then we realized it was most likely Covid), they disappeared for about five days and then slowly crept their way back. I am relieved for the obvious reasons I stated before. Unfortunately, my mother is not feeling very well and has just tested positive.

September 30

We had our party, and it was a huge success. My senses of taste and smell have almost fully returned, which is a relief to say the least. We had a large tent erected over most of the back garden that held two bars, with keepers, one for cocktails, courtesy of the generous folks at Diageo, and one for wine, beer, and water, gifted by the folks at San Pellegrino. (I am a very lucky fellow.) Sushi by our friend Makiko was passed around as canapés, and a couple of hours later, a Neapolitan pizzaiolo from Pizza Pilgrims churned out gorgeous pies from our outdoor pizza oven. Besides our wedding, we have never thrown a party on such a scale, and everyone was thrilled, as was I. But even though I was so happy to have this eclectic group of family and friends together, I think the vestiges of Covid made me more tired than normal and I could feel my body trying to drag my mind to bed. Also, I barely ate (which is a terrible habit I have at parties and must change), but what I tasted of the sushi and the pizza was fantastic. At one a.m. Millie woke up, and I swiftly took her back to bed and promptly fell asleep beside her. Felicity told me she had to oust the die-hard stragglers at two thirty a.m.

Perhaps the best result of the party besides the fun was that the pizzaiolo showed me how to use the pizza oven I basically gave up on using about two years ago because I couldn't figure out how to regulate the temperature properly (particularly of the cooking surface), and I kept burning every pizza I slid into it. He also taught me to throw a little salt on the floor of the oven to create a barrier that won't burn, like polenta or flour does, just before I put in a pizza. So simple and it works.

October 1

This morning we cleaned up a bit, then we lolled about the rest of the day. Having eaten very little the night before, as I said, this is what I ate:

8:30 a.m.: Star pasta with butter, Parmigiano, and scrambled egg

10:30 a.m.: Leftover minestrone with a piece of toast

1:30 p.m.: Toasted pita bread stuffed with sheep's cheese, tomato, and sautéed peppers and onions

4:00 p.m.: An espresso (to pick me up for a workout)

5:00 to 6:00 p.m. (shared between Fee, me, and the kids): I fired up the pizza oven and made a couple of classic pizza margheritas, a plain pizza with sautéed peppers and onions slathered with goat cheese, and focaccia with EVOO and rock salt.

The pizza turned out beautifully, which does not often happen. I attribute this to the expert coaching of the pizzaiolo who made the pizzas the night before.

After watching a dreadful film with the kids, we made it an early night.

October 2

As I had Italian sausages and British beef mince soon to expire in the fridge, I put them to good use. I made a quick Bolognese with the mince, extracted the sausage meat from its casing, and sautéed it with broccoli rabe. This will be tossed with orecchiette tomorrow for the photographer Matt Holyoak and his team, who are coming to shoot some content for San Pellegrino. I also made chicken stock and chicken meatballs that would feature in the photos.

For dinner Felicity and I ate the Bolognese with penne. It was good, I must admit.

October 3

Matt and his crew arrived, and we filmed and photographed the San Pellegrino stuff. My daughter Isabel, who is now starting to work regularly as a makeup artist, did her best to make me look presentable. When we finished, I served the orecchiette with sausage and broccoli rabe. I also made a very light marinara that could be integrated into the sausage dish if people chose to. Everyone went back for seconds, which means it was successful.

While they broke down the photo equipment, Isabel and I went to Matteo's football match at the school. It was fun and painful to watch, like most football matches with kids under the age of ten. We walked Matteo home and then I headed to J. Sheekey to meet Felicity. We shared a dozen oysters and had martinis. As we were still hungry, I ordered the prawn tempura and Felicity the sea bass tartare. After this light repast we headed to see our friend Andrew Scott in a one-man interpretation of my favorite play, *Uncle Vanya*.

It was brilliant. I knew Andrew was good, but I mean . . . really. Can someone be *too good* at something? I mean so good that everyone else who does that same thing should just stop doing it because what's the fucking point? That's how good he was. Is. Always will be. I hate him. I love him. I hate him. If I find out he can cook, I'm hurling myself into the Thames.

October 5

My father is back home from the hospital, completely recovered and in good form, as they say. My mother is much better as well and says she feels like she just has a cold. I am thankful. We cannot prove that I gave my parents the dreaded virus, but considering the fact that I met hundreds of people in New York before visiting them, coupled with my flulike symptoms, it is more than likely that I was the culprit. Had they been compromised for the long term or worse (died), how could I have ever forgiven myself? I don't want to think of it because I have thought of it too often this last week. Anyway, all is well, and my sister Gina is there looking after them brilliantly but dreading she will catch it herself. Fingers crossed her good deed goes unpunished.

Tonight, Felicity, Lottie, and my branding agent, Amanda Bross, and I ate at a rather fancy sushi place that was delicious. Afterward we went to an event celebrating the reopening of the Harrods food hall, which has just been restored to its original 1903 grandeur and then some. I didn't really get a chance to look around because I got way-laid by a couple of reporters who asked far too many questions about things unrelated to food and Harrods. As I was about to make my way through the shiny new room, two guys came up to me and intro-duced themselves. They have a company that delivers premade meals to your home and reminded me that they had sent me some samples several years back in the hopes that I might sign on to promote them. I told them that I did remember, and they asked why I didn't sign on and I politely told them, "It just wasn't for me." I did not tell them that I didn't like their product and I feared that if they realized their hopes of expanding their business, the quality of the product would most likely decline, thus making it even *more* unpalatable to me. But instead of just saying something like "Well, it was nice to meet you" and moving on, they remained, standing too close to me the way pushy people do, and kept insisting that I should be their spokesperson because their business is huge now and didn't I just want to come over right now and have a taste because it was so good! I told them as politely as possible that I didn't want to sample their wares because I'd just finished a large meal. Unfortunately, it was only after taking too many cringeworthy photos together (even though a compatriot of theirs had been documenting the whole torturous exchange on her iPhone not so surreptitiously) that they eventually went away.

Soon afterward, as we started to leave, a chef introduced himself to me, and believe it or not, he was the chef who worked with the two fellows who wouldn't take no for an answer. What a shock! Of course, they instantly appeared out of nowhere and insisted again that I try their product. I finally acquiesced because at this point, I was afraid they'd follow me home if I didn't, so I tasted it. I took more uncomfortable photos with them, which, along with the myriad others taken earlier, they could plaster shamelessly all over their social media as a way of implying that I am a rabid fan of their work.

I hate people like that, and as I get older, I am finding it increasingly difficult to decline their advances with politeness. Not that they would know what politeness is anyway.

On the way home in the cab, Felicity and Lottie both complained of stomach cramps. I was fine, however, and slept very well until about six a.m., when *my* stomach cramps began. Luckily, it was fleeting for us all, but I don't think we will be returning to that fancy sushi place. I might also add another security camera in case the pair of pushy pre-prepared-meal prima donnas try to insinuate themselves into my life yet again.

October 12

Went to Cornwall with Millie and Matteo and stayed in a hotel we'd stayed in before, right on the beach, which is perfect for families, but overall, the food left a lot to be desired. I'm looking forward to being back home and cooking for myself.

But the time spent at the hotel and on the beach was wonderful as usual. We went on a "rock pool ramble" one day. This outing was run by a company of locals, young marine biologists, and students. They take families to some of the beaches in Cornwall and teach them about the sea life in the millions of rock pools on the shores. They have also created a program that offers beach outings to the underprivileged and homeless communities there. One of the students told us that so many underprivileged people living in rural Cornwall, the poorest county in England, have never been to the shore even though they may live less than twenty miles inland. We explored the rock pools on a beach about a fifteen-minute drive from the hotel. Matteo was in heaven. Millie did her best to keep up, which was not easy as it was a blustery day and the rocks we traversed were as lethally sharp as the billions of barnacles that coated them. After an hour or so combing the rock pools, we ate bacon sandwiches and took refuge from the wind next to one of the rock outcroppings, and did our best to keep the sand from blowing into the food and our mouths.

Soon afterward we made our way back to the hotel. As we were soaked and chilled to the bone, we took much-needed hot showers, dressed, then sat by the windows and wondered which way the tide was flowing.

Watching children play on a beach is one of the most beautiful and moving things one can ever experience, especially as one ages. Their ability to remain focused on digging a hole, then gathering seawater in a pail and carrying it back to that hole and pouring it in, watching the sand absorb it before running back to refill the pail and do it all over again. Why is it so fascinating to watch? Because it is free of any affectation. It is unburdened. It is pure in its gesture and intent. And what is that intent? To fill with water a hole that can never be filled. But they don't know that. Or maybe they do, and they just don't care. An adult would care and figure out a way to keep the sand from absorbing the water. But then what? The game is over. Where's the fun in that?

The next morning, we made waffles in the little kitchenette that serves the rooms in that part of the hotel. The children devoured them. I decided I would buy them a waffle maker for Christmas.

Felicity and I watched the latest documentary about David Beckham, which is wonderful. In the last episode we see Beckham in a heavenly outdoor cooking facility. It is a paradise of grills, griddles, stoves, rotisseries, cutting boards, and all the utensils that any culinary obsessive needs. My dream. I've decided we will be friends whether Becks likes it or not.

We had such a lovely time, as we always do in Cornwall, but unfortunately on this trip the food left a lot to be desired. For me that is always a struggle. One of the restaurants in the hotel had a menu with a dish from practically every country around the globe, especially those that use lots of spice. Unfortunately, the chef had no knowledge of how to cook any of them well, or at least with any subtlety. I won't even discuss the selection and execution of pasta dishes for fear it might depress me so much that I'd need to take to my bed for the rest of the day. To me cooking, acting, and directing are all related. A good director of film or theater is felt rather than seen. By this I mean there is a clarity of vision and an assured aesthetic, but the focus is the truth of the story through the performances and the imagery. When it comes to acting, if people see a performance that they admire they often say, "It was like she wasn't even acting." Ideally, we should say the same about a good director. Everything the director has done is up there on the screen or the stage, but it should seem as though what we're watching was born by itself. A virgin birth. A creative immaculate conception.

In my opinion a good chef's food must be the same. The chef must not be present. Only the food. This holds true not only for the preparation of classic dishes but especially for new ones. If a chef takes certain ingredients, combines them, and prepares them in a singular way, the result must work effortlessly without a trace of imposition or even thought. It must seem that the dish came into being because it was just meant to be. Like true love. Unfortunately, neither is easy to find. Nonetheless, we continue the search.

October 14

Received news that the green light for the new *Is Stanley Tucci Still in Italy?* show has been put on hold until Disney management has had a chance to go over the budget. We are not the only production this is happening to; it is across the board. They have already canceled over forty shows, and this is a clear sign that they will cancel more. Fingers crossed that ours is not among them.

This now makes what was already a tight schedule even worse. We were to film one episode before Christmas, edit it in the new year while we prepped the remaining nine, then film them, making changes as necessary based on our assessment of episode one. We planned to begin shooting in March and continue until the end of July. However, it's more than likely that we won't be green-lit until January, which makes that schedule impossible. Well, best-laid plans and all that, I guess.

I'm sick to my stomach about it, as I have other work in August and the fall I've committed to, and if the show in Italy is pushed later it might conflict with them, causing me to postpone it for another year. But given the fragile and confused state of show business now, those projects may also never come to fruition. I must find a new line of work. Maybe I'll become a chef. There's an easy life.

October 16

We arrived home in the afternoon after a slightly delayed train ride, unpacked, exercised, and fed the kids. I made pasta marinara with mushrooms as I was craving pasta with any sauce, having not eaten it for almost five days, which is practically a record for me. We were in bed early as Felicity has to leave tomorrow morning for the Cotswolds to "work," and Matteo is having his tonsils out and we wanted him to get a good night's rest. And we wanted one as well.

October 17

Twenty minutes on the bike and a TRX workout compelled me to eat more pasta marinara with the addition of scrambled eggs in the morning. Soon afterward I took Matteo to the hospital. We played guessing games in the car ("I'm thinking of an animal, I'm thinking of a tree, a body of water," and so on), which proved yet again that at the age of eight and a half his knowledge and vocabulary are staggeringly advanced.

He had not eaten since ten that morning, nor would he be able to until after his operation, which was scheduled for four that afternoon, but he never complained. He also didn't show the slightest bit of nervousness.

He was wheeled into pre-op, where he was asked to look at a Where's Waldo? book to distract him from having his fluids and anesthesia administered, and his huge, beautiful eyes closed within seconds of it coursing through his narrow veins. I ran across the street to buy a miso soup and some dumplings, because I was famished. (I was back in the room in less than five minutes, for any of you who think I was being a neglectful parent.)

Half an hour later, after a successful operation, my younger son was very groggy but very soon ate four chocolate chip cookies and some ice cream. Then he fell fast asleep again.

He was discharged a couple of hours later, and when we arrived home Millie had written a "hope you feel better" note for him illustrated with rainbows and hearts. When he walked in the door her eyes locked on him. I could see her looking for profound changes that might have taken place in her big brother, but other than extreme grogginess and a tender throat, there were none. They both watched a bit of television while he ate two bowls of pastina with butter and cheese, Millie ate a heaping portion of mixed berries, and I of course ate more pasta, but this time with broccoli, sautéed garlic, Parmigiano, and a dusting of sweet paprika.

I didn't want Matteo to sleep alone, which meant I couldn't let Millie sleep alone (that would have been cruel), so we all slept in my bed, which means they slept, but I didn't. Because our bedroom faces the street and the ambient light kept us from sleeping well, Felicity and I had blackout blinds installed while we were away last week. (Why it took us six years to get around to it I will never know.) I told the kids that it was going to be darker than usual when I turned out the light. Millie was thrilled and shouted, "*Yes, I cannot wait to see the darkness!*" My little existentialist.

During our brief stay in the hospital, I received the good news that the *Stan Goes Through Italy Yet Again* show would indeed move forward as planned. I know that my representatives pulled many strings to make that happen and I am grateful. This is an enormous relief given the undulating landscape of eggshells that Hollywood is built on these days. Strikes, quickly evolving technology, attempts to create competitive and successful streaming platforms, corporate restructuring, and substantial financial losses have thrown Tinseltown into confusion, thus affecting hundreds of projects and tens of thousands of livelihoods. One can only hope things get sorted out soon without too many people losing too much.

October 18

Matteo is still a bit ragged but doing well and eating just fine. His friend Catalina, whom he has not seen in a while, has come over to spend some time with him. I'm so happy that they have come up with a way to remove tonsils so efficiently without the pain and ten-day recovery of days gone by.

I am very lucky to have five beautiful, kind, intelligent, and funny children. Like most people, they have their likes and dislikes when it comes to food. Matteo will not go near an avocado or a raw tomato, but Millie will devour both. Isabel to this day cannot stand the smell or taste of parsley, and Camilla prefers vegetables to meat, but Nicolo must be reminded to cease eating meat and cheese and have something green every now and again. They all love Italian food, of course, and have a real understanding of what good-quality Italian food is, which might make them a bit snobby but frankly that's better than the opposite. I think about their "Italianness" a lot. I see traces of both sides of my family in them. Matteo has hair similar to what mine once was, but his is darker; Camilla's eyes are practically black like mine; Isabel has light brown eyes and a few freckles like my mother; Nicolo has the dark eyebrows and slim features that my father had as a young man; and Millie (née Emilia) has piercing brown eyes and my olive skin and physique. Luckily most of their physical makeup and intelligence have been gifted to them by their respective mothers, both beautiful and extremely bright women.

Comprising a variety of southern Mediterranean and northern European genes, my children are each singularly stunning in their own way. But if there are two *behavioral* traits that exemplify "Italianness," Millie might be the most "Italian" of them all, these traits being the age-old clichés of how Italians cannot talk without using their hands and how they're able to speak volumes with a single subtle gesture or a glance. (Clichés exist for a reason: because they stem from some kind of truth. It's when a cliché is used to denigrate that it becomes untrue.) When Millie tells a story (especially if the story is about something someone has done that has offended her, which can take quite a while, as anyone with a five-year-old knows), she cannot do so without a series of exacting hand and arm movements that involuntarily punctuate her words. They are slightly stiff, emphatic gestures that one might normally see used by a Roman college professor passionately explaining the importance of his subject to unruly students, an Umbrian who has taken umbrage with the way a chef has prepared his or her *porchetta*, or a Neapolitan driver trying to make the traffic cop understand that streetlights *are merely a suggestion.* When not ranting about her fickle friends, Millie is equally as "Italian" when she feels that she has been slighted. When this happens, she simply lowers her gaze, glares at the culprit with those dark eyes of hers, and ocularly speaks tomes of threats in a heartbeat. She must have just a little bit more of the Italian DNA that causes this behavior to come so naturally to her. Coupled with an upper-middle-class British accent and wrapped in a tiny little five-year-old body, her impassioned tales of complaint and "if looks could kill" stares are a sight to behold. And yet this is a child who won't eat *pasta con pomodoro.*

October 23

We spent the day preparing for and throwing a dinner party. Our friend Sam Rockwell is in town. I love Sam Rockwell. We have known each other for over thirty years but it's only in the last five or so that we have reconnected, because he's been filming different projects in London. I cannot tell you what a joy it has been to have him here. He is ridiculously talented, brilliantly funny, and kind of heart. Leslie Bibb, his partner of many years, ain't so bad either. We also invited Saoirse Ronan and her partner, Jack. Sam brought a makeup artist he and Saoirse know from a film they did together a couple of years ago. I have known Saoirse since she was thirteen years old, when we worked on *The Lovely Bones*. We have crossed paths periodically and emailed as well, but tonight was the first time we've had a dinner together. I'd promised her I would make risotto and so I did. I also made chicken cacciatore.

A few days earlier I ran into a fellow not far from our house who told me that he supplied all the Italian produce for our mutual friend, the great chef Gennaro Contaldo, and that he would like to send me some. Greedily, I said yes.

A few days later a huge box brimming with purple artichokes, mozzarella, eggplant, zucchini, *puntarelle*, forty-two-month-aged Parmigiano, *pomodorini*, *pane carasau*, radicchio di Treviso, Ligurian pesto, sweet Calabrian onions, truffle paste, clementines, red apples, Amalfi lemons, and other Italian goodies arrived. It was overwhelming and thrilling. I realize now that a cornucopia of gorgeous produce is all

I want to find under the tree with my name on it come Christmas morning.

We put some of that produce to good use for the party. Felicity busied herself with the apples making a tarte Tatin while I steamed the artichokes and prepared the chicken. Felicity and I do work very well together in the kitchen. Given how much time we spend there, that's a good thing, otherwise we would have divorced years ago. She is much better at making dishes that need to be baked or roasted, and I am more comfortable working on the stovetop. She is also brilliant at making dough for pizza or pasta, whereas I struggle with both, but I pride myself in making whatever sauce we've decided to pair them with, extremely well. Time cooking with someone you love is time well spent.

We were quite behind schedule when Sam texted that he had mentioned to another mutual friend and his wife that he was coming to our house for dinner and perhaps they should join. (I adore him but he has a habit of doing this.) Felicity and I thought about what we were making and assessed whether there was enough. We decided that there was, but the problem was that I had already promised Saoirse I would make risotto, and making an extra two portions, which is really four portions because I always assume people will want seconds, is not an easy thing. Also, our mutual friend and his wife are vegan. Even though they had offered to bring their own food, we insisted that we would and could adapt accordingly. We had already made chicken stock for the risotto, which we couldn't use for the vegan version, so now we needed to make a vegetable stock, which Felicity swiftly did. Cooking two pots of risotto simultaneously is not recommended but one does what one must in a pinch.

The kitchen was a mess, the children were unbathed and unfed, we were still in our exercise gear from the morning's workout (gross), no appetizers had been prepared, and the table had yet to be set. Sam then texted and said he and his friend would be arriving early. I told him that he was not allowed to arrive early as we had too much to do because he had expanded the guest list at the eleventh hour, and I firmly suggested he go to a bar and get a drink. He then texted us from the car that it was raining (*WTF?! He was in a car!*), and I told him it doesn't rain inside bars, and he should find one posthaste, get a f—ing drink, and stay there until the appointed time of the dinner. Actors.

In case you haven't gleaned, when throwing a dinner party, I am one who likes things to be *just so* when guests arrive. Felicity is very much the same. The table should be set, the house as clean and tidy as possible, lighting adjusted, candles lit, music playing, appetizers laid out, wine opened, and the bar stocked for me to make at least martinis and Negronis. Unfortunately, with an hour to go, we were a long way from that point.

So, I quickly made martinis for us both, we shifted gears, and by the time Sam sheepishly arrived with his lovely friend, we were somehow as ready as a harried couple could be. Saoirse and Jack arrived minutes later, only to be followed by Woody Harrelson and his lovely wife, Laura. I was so happy to see Woody (one of my favorite actors and one of the funniest people ever), as it had been over six years, and finally get to meet his very charming wife.

Saoirse is now a young woman, poised, articulate, kind, and, as we know, absurdly talented. She has also become interested in cooking, which makes me so pleased, and we promised to cook together soon. It's disconcerting to me because it seems that not so long ago, she had just turned thirteen. Now she is in her late twenties. How did that happen? Where did all that time go? The way time treats us and the way we use time is different for everyone. Some become wise with age and others stay perpetually naïve. Then there are those like Saoirse who were born with a wisdom beyond their years. During the filming of

The Lovely Bones there finally came the day when we were to shoot the scene where my character lures her character into his underground lair and, although it is never shown, rapes and kills her. I was very nervous about filming the scene and I asked the director, Peter Jackson, to film it as simply and as quickly as possible. At first her character is intrigued by the trinkets and baubles that decorate the space and sees my character as a kind man. Then in a moment she realizes that the opposite is true and attempts to escape, at which point I grab her forcefully. As I said, the scene went no further than that because the outcome is obvious. But doing *just that* made me terribly uncomfortable, and after every take I would ask Saoirse, "Are you okay?" And after every take she would shrug and say, "Yeah, I'm fine!" and smile happily. At the end of what I believe was the third or fourth take, I asked her yet again, "Sersh, are you okay?" But instead of her usual answer, this time she looked me straight in the eyes and said in that cool Dublin accent, "Stanley, I'm okay. The question is, are *you* okay?" I learned a great deal about not only acting but life that day, from a thirteen-year-old.

Much time has passed since then. I am now in my sixties and Saoirse is a young woman. But for me, as for so many of us, time is something to which we are always trying to catch up. Saoirse Ronan will always be waiting for time to catch up to her.

How good the food was tonight I can't really say, but people seemed to enjoy it. All I know is that we had a truly great time as we ate, and happily drank the delicious wine they had all brought with them, into the wee hours. Those untethered thespians finding home in each other within our home once again. I wouldn't have it any other way. I'd only ask for a little more notice next time (Sam).

October 25–26

Moldova.

Lottie and I went with UNHCR (the United Nations High Commissioner for Refugees) to meet with the staff and Ukrainian refugees for two days. It was my first "mission" with them. To say that I was humbled is an understatement.

On our first day in Moldova, we drove to the Mimi winery. Built in the late nineteenth century, it was expanded in the 1930s and then again just recently. The newest renovations were stunning. Low-profile glass and dark steel, the contemporary structures created a dramatic counterpoint to the grand old buildings that already existed. We were brought there to meet and cook with a group of Ukrainian women and hear their stories. Svetlana, the chef who oversaw the making of the meal, cooked at a primary school in Ukraine before she fled over the border with her two daughters. She now cooks in a primary school in Moldova, her husband having chosen to stay behind.

In the kitchen that evening, there was a total of six women from their midthirties to their fifties, from every walk of life. All had children of different ages who had come with them, and some had husbands who had fled with them as well. A couple of them were divorced and some had husbands who had remained in Ukraine for various reasons. But no matter what their individual circumstances were, when I spoke to them about their current situation, it was clear that life was not easy and that they all longed for home.

However, as we cooked together, slicing potatoes, cabbage, carrots, celery, garlic, onions, and beetroot that would soon become a hearty borscht when cooked in a beef broth that Svetlana had made earlier that morning, they were anything but sad, or at least they hid their sadness very well. They made fun of my clumsiness when I rolled the dough balls that would blossom into buttery garlic-covered buns to be served alongside the borscht and joked about everything, including each other.

The American ambassador to Moldova, Kent Logsdon, and his wife, Michelle, arrived as the kitchen was in full swing. Everyone was happy to see them as they have been involved in making sure the Moldovan government had and continues to have any support it needs to resettle the Ukrainians as efficiently and comfortably as possible. I can't imagine a better duo to have in that office during a very complex time. They were warm and open and devoted to making sure that Moldova is on the path to a much-longed-for EU membership.

After the borscht and buns were ready, we sat in the winery's spacious restaurant. The tables were filled with platters of cheeses, meats, and vegetable appetizers, and the gorgeous wine from the vineyard was opened.

Through a translator, I chatted with Svetlana about food, her daughters, and her yearning to go to Italy, especially Rome. She explained that she was obsessed with the city and in her spare time has done paintings of it. She says that Rome is calling her. When we spoke about her husband, she told me that he had refused to come, insisting that Ukraine was his home and that he would never leave. I asked her what she personally wanted most of all and she told me through sudden tears that all she wanted was to return home.

I also talked with Julia, who spoke English very well, having had her own international business in Ukraine before the war. Besides being extremely funny, she was articulate and described how hard it was to be in Moldova, especially as a divorced woman with an eight-year-old son. When they first arrived in Moldova, she thought he was adjusting, but after a while he started to change. Nowadays he often packs his rucksack and tells her that he's ready to return home. She then tells him that what he wants is not possible. Then, a few days later, he will repeat the same thing and she must repeat the same words. How often can a parent tell a child that their dream cannot come true before both begin to unravel?

Every refugee I spoke to had basically the same story to tell in one form or another. Luckily, they were able to escape to a country that welcomed them and from which they could even visit their homes and loved ones from time to time when it was safe enough to do so.

Moldova is a huge wine-producing country. Most of the production used to go to Russia or countries within the Soviet bloc, but since the end of the Cold War it has been sold elsewhere. America has given grants to help bolster wine production and it has paid off. A Moldovan wine won a gold medal in Paris last year. The country also has wonderful food, with mostly a Slavic bent but vegetable-forward. This is because 75 percent of the soil in Moldova is incredibly rich and the land is primarily flat, making it easy to cultivate. The produce I saw at farm stands as we traveled to and from our meetings was extraordinary. Dark red grapes, deep purple plums, squash, tomatoes, cucumbers, and cherries galore, and the local dishes that are created with all that produce were a revelation. We went to two superb, very affordable restaurants, the first being Fuior. This is what we ate:

Jellied rabbit, with horseradish

Chicken liver pâté

Roasted peppers stuffed with cream cheese

Three types of lard (don't remember how they differed, only that they were great)

Mashed beans with onion chips

Eggplant rolls with walnuts

A variety of savory placinte (fried pastries stuffed with cheese, potatoes, cabbage, etc.)

Black dumplings (squid ink) stuffed with white fish

Pork stew with mamaliga (polenta)

Green salad with mustard greens

I can't remember what wine we had but we drank both red and white, and they were delicious. Although certain dishes were reminiscent of a lot of Slavic and even Italian food I've had before, they were all new to me and I couldn't get enough of them. I wanted to return to Fuior the next night, but it was suggested by one of the team that we go to Julien, a French-inspired bistro about a ten-minute walk away.

Upon entering Julien, we were ushered into a small, curtain-enclosed lounge in the back of the restaurant, where we were seated on cushioned banquettes and small armchairs around an eclectic mix of beautifully set antique tables. When the chef/owner, a jolly thirty-year-old Moldovan native named Dmitri, entered, he turned borscht red when he saw me. He said that he was a huge fan of the Italy show, that it had been a dream of his to meet me, and that he was now so nervous that he was almost afraid to cook for me. I was more than flattered and told him that he needn't be nervous at all and that I was so excited to be cooked for by him, as were we all.

He took a deep breath and told us where he had previously worked (in Michelin-starred Parisian restaurants) and, more important, why he cooked. He said that like so many chefs, he wanted to re-create the aromas, the flavors, the warmth, and the conviviality that he experienced in the kitchen and the dining room of his family home. He got a bit choked up as he spoke about his grandfather, whom he loved and who had taught him so much, and we got choked up as well. He asked why we were in Moldova, and when we told him we were with UNHCR, he said that he had taken Ukrainian families into his home at the beginning of the war and that he now employs Ukrainians in his restaurant. We toasted him with a delicate sparkling wine that had been served to us as a welcoming drink, and then he disappeared into the kitchen, only to return a moment later to recommend a white and a red to accompany the meal—a meal that was extraordinary.

A selection of appetizers described as a "tasting set" was first:

Deviled eggs

A rustic terrine

Profiteroles with trout

Mamaliga chips

Grape rolls (grape leaves) stuffed with meat

A variety of small pies

We were all silenced by how good it was.

While we gluttonized, Dmitri reentered pushing a cart on top of which was displayed a glorious dark-aged tomahawk steak, and a piece of pork that had been salted, coated in herbs, and aged for two weeks. He told us that both cuts of meat were from animals raised in Moldova, and that he cooks them first on the grill, then in a pan, and serves them family style. We ordered both. And both were incredible. The beef was rich and tender, and the pork—which was such a dark red, one never would have thought it had once been a pig—literally melted *before* you put it in your mouth. Dmitri's face borschted again when we applauded his undeniable talent at the end of the meal.

Afterward we gathered in the main dining area and Dmitri locked the door. He stood on a chair (we were forewarned that he does this often) and told us and the other customers that it was time for a party. From his precarious pulpit he spoke about the importance of food, of love, of his grandfather, and told us that we must drink, dance on the bar, and do whatever we wanted to do because we should "live in this moment." He started to cry toward the end of his speech, but after composing himself, he exhorted us to enjoy life because "tomorrow is an illusion!" Unfortunately Dimitri is more than right.

When you look at the mindless repetition of suffering in the world, even a glimmer of hope is hard to find. Human beings need one another because we can give each other so much, especially hope, but we often forget this. Just look at the way we treat each other.

We also need the earth and what it gives us, but we often forget this too. Just look at the way we treat it.

Yet the two are inextricably linked. Communing with one another with what is given to us by the earth, meaning its bounty, is one of the most crucial components of the life cycle. This communion can ameliorate, unite, elate, stave off conflicts, and create long-lasting bonds of friendship and of love.

Is it a panacea for the horror we sow?

No. I'm not suggesting it is.

But it's something.

It helps.

Yes, hope is hard to find, but it can often be found at the table.

And tables are easy to build.

The weather was cool and crisp as we walked back to the hotel along the peaceful streets lined with trees in full autumnal hues. Yet only a short drive away over the border there was a place where no peace was to be found. But in Moldova, on that night, in that moment, there was peace. And there still is. At least for now.

October 28–29

This weekend we stayed at home with the kids. We went to the farmers' market, which was filled with all of my favorite fall produce. We bought pumpkins and set to working on them. Carving pumpkins is the only thing I like about Halloween, because to me, the rest of it is a parent's nightmare. What, may I ask, is appealing or even at all *right* about a holiday where fear and horror are the overriding themes, and your children wander around in the dark going to the houses of strangers begging for candy? Who the f— ever thought this was a good idea or even necessary? I can assure you that it wasn't me.

October 31

Lottie and I went to Sabor with our friend and colleague Matt Ball. Matt was second camera for most of the last two seasons of *Searching for Italy* and we have asked him to take the helm as director of photography going forward. He is talented, kind, smart, and funny, appreciates food, and knows how to cook. He also shoots Ina Garten's show in America, which his wife directs. When I did Ina's show last year, it was such a pleasure to spend time with him in a much more relaxed setting than we are used to when filming in Italy.

Today at Sabor we ordered white wine, *croquetas* with goat cheese, squid fettuccine (squid cut to resemble the pasta) with a Manchego sauce, peppers stuffed with goat cheese, monkfish tempura, *presa iberica* with salsa verde, gem lettuce with *bottarga*, and Manchego and hazelnuts. I have no words for it. You'll just have to go yourself.

It was Halloween, a holiday of which, as I've already made clear, I am not a fan. Felicity and Isabel took the kids out and I opted to stay home and man the door. It ended up being quite a busy night. Children of all ages showed up for tricks or treats and my heart softened a bit. Especially when the littlest ones of the lot asked politely. I actually teared up at one point. Ugh!! What is happening? Emotionally moved by Halloween. Christ. Okay, I must admit that I still have a photo of a very young Nicolo, Isabel, and Camilla dressed for Halloween as the Marx Brothers and it breaks my heart every time I look at it. But I must say that what is even more heartbreaking is that out of the countless houses we went to that night, only one person recognized who they were dressed as. Only *one guy* knew who the Marx Brothers were! I realized then that Halloween was becoming worse than ever, and that cinema was dead.

November 1

Gave a talk with Mary McCartney and Ruth Rogers to promote Mary's new cookbook, in which we are both featured. Afterward I went straight home and had a bowl of pasta by the light of the fridge.

November 2

I wrote at home for a bit and then felt the need to cook. Because I am bored of making myself the same things repeatedly, I decided that each week I will make at least one new recipe to bulk out my culinary repertoire. As the weather has been getting chillier, I thought something warming would be appropriate, so I opted for a shepherd's pie. I had only made it a couple of times before, which seems silly since it's not that hard and I absolutely love it. However, I chose to make not a true shepherd's pie (which is made with lamb, something I learned when I moved to England) but a *cottage* pie, which is made with beef (which in America we would still call a shepherd's pie).

Anyway, I set to work and was able to finish my humble British fare just as the kids returned home from school. After helping with a bit of homework, I left them with our nanny and scooted off to Matteo's parent-teacher conferences alone as Felicity was ostensibly out at a "book launch." (I hate to say anything, but she has more launches than Cape Canaveral.) Anyway, after the conferences, where I proudly received glowing comments about Matteo from every teacher, I returned home to make sausages with rice and peas for the children's dinner while I warmed up the cottage pie. When it was ready, I offered them a piece to accompany their meal, which they unapologetically declined. Slightly insulted but unfazed, I ate a large portion of the thing by myself, complemented by a guzzle of a superb red Mercurey. Although a bit undersalted, the cottage pie hit the spot, and for a moment, I pitied my children's palates as I watched them gorge on the charred, shriveled intestines of a pig.

Someday, I mused silently, *someday you will come to understand the culinary lion who stands before you, and you will rue the day you declined even a crumb of the gustatory offerings from his generous, loving heart and his scarred, gifted hands.*

I was roused from my self-aggrandizing reverie by a tiny voice asking, "When's Mummy coming home?"

Philistines.

November 3

Met Isabel and Nico at the White Cube gallery, where we saw a stunning exhibition of paintings by Marina Rheingantz, then headed straight to Sabor yet again because I know that they both love it, especially Nico. We ordered a huge amount of food because like their father, they are both voracious. Nico has lost about ten pounds due to the long hours and effort that working as a chef in a top restaurant demands. He has never been so happy.

November 4

After a punishing power yoga session with Monique (the woman is inhuman), sticking with my resolution to make new dishes every week, I decided to make borscht. I had made it only once many years ago, because I love it and I miss the days when I could go to the Carnegie Deli and order a bowl. So, inspired by Svetlana and all the Ukrainian women I met the week before in Moldova, I set to work while the children ran around the house and Felicity somehow managed to read the paper amid the din. Here's how I did it:

Borscht

Glug of olive oil or vegetable oil
1 teaspoon butter (optional)
2 carrots, roughly grated, then finely chopped
2 celery stalks, finely chopped
2 medium onions, finely chopped
2 garlic cloves, finely chopped
5 medium beets, peeled and washed, roughly grated, then coarsely chopped
2 medium potatoes, washed and peeled, roughly grated, then coarsely chopped
Coarse salt
Freshly ground black pepper

6½ cups beef stock (your own or store-bought)
White wine vinegar
Sour cream or plain creamy yogurt (optional)

- Drizzle the oil and put the butter (if using) into a 5-quart Dutch oven over medium heat.
- When the oil is hot, add the carrots, celery, onions, and garlic and cook until soft. Then add the beets and potatoes and stir. Season with salt and pepper and let cook for 5 or so minutes, stirring now and then. When the beets and potatoes have started to soften a bit, add the beef stock and more salt and pepper. Bring to a boil for a minute or so and then reduce the heat to low. Cover and cook for 45 minutes, stirring occasionally, then add 2 to 3 capfuls of white wine vinegar, stir, taste, and add more salt and pepper if needed. If desired, serve with a dollop of sour cream or a plain creamy yogurt of your choice.
- Borscht can be eaten hot or cold.

We ate this over the next three days. Twice for breakfast. It was good. Very. And cleansing. *Very.*

The SAG strike is finally over. Thank God. Now the studios are making up for lost time by sending actors on endless junkets to promote films in the hopes of securing as many nominations as possible for the absurd number of awards that Hollywood adorns itself with every year. If the money spent on press junkets and award campaigns were spent making good films, it would be so much better for everyone, especially moviegoers.

November 11

It was my sixty-third birthday. Matteo and Millie made me cards and we spent the day at home. Felicity gave me a beautiful sweater. I assembled a six-by-four-foot soccer goal for Matteo to use in the garden. He proceeded to batter it with balls for the rest of the afternoon. The night was too much fun. Woody and Laura; Sam and Leslie; Piper Perabo; Matt Damon and his wife, Lucy; and Jamie Dornan all came over for drinks, after which our boisterous group headed to Riva for a dinner that Felicity had planned. We ate prosciutto, *puntarelle*, langoustines, risotto with white truffle, and salad. The more wine that was had, the louder our table became, and then came the speeches, which were flattering and funny. The rest of the customers, including a woman named Alexandra, were in shock at seeing this cluster of celebrities in a small local restaurant. As I made my way around the restaurant apologizing to each table, I chatted with Alexandra and her husband, both teachers, who were there to celebrate her birthday as well. The table of cheap hams that were my friends rose to their feet instantly when they discovered it was Alexandra's birthday and gave a far-too-loud rousing chorus of you-know-what. I think the staff couldn't wait for us to leave.

November 13

Had dinner at a Japanese restaurant with Lottie and Martina, who was the kids' nanny until she moved back to Slovakia a couple of years ago. We devoured our food. It's no wonder. Afterward I met the chef, who was from New Zealand, and he told me he had once been the head chef at Nobu in London.

Afterward I moderated a Q and A for Matthew Heineman's film *American Symphony*. I had watched the film the day before to prepare for the Q and A. It's yet another beautiful documentary by this supremely talented man. The film shows a well-known musician's career as it is becoming more successful and exciting. He is nominated for eleven Grammys as he is preparing for a Carnegie Hall performance of his composition *American Symphony*. At the same time, his wife's health is declining as she undergoes a brutal bone marrow transplant and chemo treatments for leukemia, which has returned after a ten-year period of remission. It's a delicately told story about the many layers of love. Love for one's work, love for one's partner, love for what love allows a person to do creatively and in life. Like all of Matthew's films, it's subtle and profound.

But I will confess that it was difficult for me to watch. Seeing the woman undergo her extreme treatment regimen and her husband doing everything he can to support her, it was like watching other people act out what Kate and I had gone through. But they weren't acting. I thought it was going to simply be a film about one man's musical prowess, which was originally Matthew's intention as well. But then as shooting began, life got in the way, and the story became a new and even deeper one. Watching her suffer, watching her husband cut her hair before she begins chemo, watching her face and body change as the side effects of the drugs slowly set in, watching him walk with her through the hospital hallways to keep up her strength, was like watching so many indelible moments during the last four years of my life with Kate, presented in an hour and a half. I will admit that I wanted to turn it off several times. But I didn't. And I'm glad I didn't. I needed to see it. Not only because Matthew had asked me to watch it and moderate a Q and A, but for other reasons. But what were those reasons? To come to terms with my survivor guilt? To put an end to my dreams? To distance myself from those memories or to keep them alive? Yes. No. Maybe.

November 14

Took the kids to the Kew Gardens Christmas lights event. We have gone for the last few years but this time we went to a preview, so there were no crowds, and it was much more enjoyable. We ate some very expensive hot dogs and sausages when we arrived, but let's just say that they were not what we were hoping for, so we discarded them after a few bites. The powdered-sugar-covered beignets were an instant hit, however. The lighting exhibitions were varied, some not very interesting, others quaintly spectacular. The small amusement fair that is constructed every year was also a hit as it contained a limited number of rides perfect for a five- and an eight-year-old. Hoping to leave swiftly after the kids had had their fair share of the fair, we somehow ended up walking almost the entire two-kilometer light trail, because we couldn't find a shortcut to the exit. We did the same thing last year. You'd think we would have learned our lesson. Eventually we found our way out and headed home, where we fed the kids pasta with pesto and ourselves some soup.

November 15

I made eggplant parmigiana with a large Italian white and purple eggplant, two British purple eggplants, and some zucchini. I left out the potatoes I normally put in. I also prepared orecchiette with sausage and broccolini for dinner, as Lottie and Martina were coming.

November 16

Tonight, I served the eggplant (or what was left after I'd made a dent in it that morning for breakfast after a workout), cooked some orzo with saffron and chicken broth, and seasoned some cod fillets that I would bake *en papillote*. Made the kids pasta with onions, butter, and peas alongside cod goujons. Millie did not complain once about the onions in the pasta, which was something like progress. I undercooked our cod fillets because I was trying to follow a recipe that I was not paying enough attention to. Felicity, Martina (who had come to stay with us for her last couple of days in London), and I ate together. She is living in Austria now, not far from her family in Slovakia. We always talk about how we hope to visit her one day and meet her parents, because like our friend Andy's family in Hungary, they make their own sausages and cured meats, grow their own vegetables, and so on. Her folks are my age but live a lifestyle more like that of my grandparents. They have their day jobs but cull from what they cultivate to create the basis of their diet. I would like the kids to experience that. Not such a bad way to live.

Matteo has also informed me that he loves carbonara. I could not be more thrilled because, as I've stated, I love it too. When made properly, carbonara is one of the greatest things you can put in your mouth. I will have to make it for him and his best friend, Arthur, who eats practically anything put in front of him. When Arthur has dinner at our house, Matteo becomes more adventurous with his eating. It's as though Arthur is his "taster," making sure that I haven't poisoned the food. Once Arthur has gobbled down his first bite and shown no sign of dying, Matteo asks if he can try a bit of what his best friend is having. Millie just watches them amused, perfectly at peace with her dinner order.

November 17

Felicity and I headed to the airport for a flight to Ireland to go to the Dingle literary festival. Last night I made us four eggplant sandwiches, which we ate in the lounge with a beer for lunch. The sauce had permeated the toasted bread, making them moreish even though they were still slightly cold. They were so much better than eating something—or *anything*—from the lounge.

November 18–19

Dingle.

Spent the weekend with colleagues/friends of Fee's, Geoff O'Sullivan and Anna Stein, as well as Yvonne McGuinness and two friends of hers, Max Porter, a brilliant author, and Mary Hickson, a producer of film and performance art. Had some fairly good food, especially at the Fish Box, a little eatery that obviously serves fish. Prior to our lunch, as we waited for our table to be free, we walked a few doors down to a small pub called Dick Mack's. It was only one of the fifty pubs in Dingle (that's one pub for every forty inhabitants), and like a number we visited, it was not only very old and very small but once was (and at times still is) a cobbler's shop. The entire interior is constructed of unpainted wood from floor to ceiling. Worn wooden counters stand on either side of the tiny room. The right-hand counter is the bar, behind which is an extraordinary display of whiskey bottles both Irish and Scottish, dating back decades. They line the shelves that snake up and around and ring the entire place. To the left is another wooden counter, into which a carbon-steel plate on carbon-steel legs is integrated, which is still used by the cobbler when he makes an appearance but is mainly used as a perch for drinkers and their drinks. Behind *this* counter the shelves are haphazardly filled with the tools and vital bric-a-brac of the cobbler's trade, some of which looked older than many of the whiskey bottles scattered around and among them.

The place reminded me of McSorley's, the oldest Irish pub in Manhattan, which I used to frequent whenever I found myself on the Lower

East Side. Opened in the mid-1800s, it was only in 1970 that McSorley's allowed women to enter its dusty den of drink, a practice more extreme than that in Ireland at the time. Yet, although Irish bars did allow women entry in those days, they were relegated to little wooden cubicles next to the bar called "snugs." Only in the snug's confessional-like structure could women socialize with one another, and only through a little confessional-like window to the bar could they receive their drinks. ("Forgive me, Father, I'll have another, and make it a double.") Dick Mack's still had one of these snugs, but fortunately women now have the choice of sitting there or any other place they fancy.

This segregation of the sexes, which still exists today in so many societies and religions, and—let's face it—too many other places, is something I have never understood. Why do men eschew the company of women in favor of the company of men? For the most part I've always found women easier to talk to, more interesting, funnier, more ironic, better listeners, and better conversationalists than most people born with penises. Is it because they're not trying to prove anything?

Anyway, after a Guinness at Dick Mack's, we headed to the Fish Box (there's a dirty joke in there somewhere, and if you find it, send it to me), where we ordered shrimp cocktail, fried fish tacos, onion rings, and fish and chips. An extremely fried lunch but extremely satisfying. The tacos were especially good, with lightly pickled red onion, lettuce, and a delicate creamy dressing. I couldn't stop eating them. But eventually I was forced to stop eating them because I'd eaten all of them.

The next day, Yvonne, Felicity, and I went for a stroll along the dramatic cliffs outside of Dingle and down to Coumeenoole Beach. It was stunningly beautiful. Almost overwhelmingly so. Afterward we drove to Kruger's, a small pub, where we had a Guinness that was even better than the one we had drunk the day before. Why does a product that is supposed to be consistent in taste and texture vary so much from pub to pub? Some Guinnesses are richer, some more viscous, some a bit thinner, and so on. I've been told that it has to do with the cleanliness or uncleanliness of the hoses and that if the tank is new, it affects the density of the liquid, and several other reasonably reasonable reasons. In the end I don't know if there is just one explanation. All I know is that when the stars are aligned and a Guinness is poured "right," there is practically nothing better.

The first time I had Guinness in the land of its origin was about twenty-five years ago in Dublin at the Guinness factory itself. I had taken a tour with a friend, who has since passed away, and at the end we were given two wooden tokens and escorted to the basement bar. Here we presented our tokens, entitling us to two half pints of the hearty stuff. I had drunk Guinness before in bars stateside but the taste of those two half pints in Dublin was something revelatory. I told my friend it was like drinking an eight-course meal, not because it was filling but because of the complexity of the flavors. The Guinness we drank with Yvonne on that blustery day tasted the same. Rich, deep, dark, joyful, melancholic, comforting; a flawless liquid fermented in history and myth.

November 22

I took a day off from exercising (I mean, how long do I really want to live?) and had a couple of early Zoom meetings in the office with Lottie, then came home and started cooking. I followed a recipe from Julius Roberts's beautiful cookbook *The Farm Table* to make *pissaladière*. Make it! I also cut an eggplant, two zucchini, one red onion, and four small potatoes into chunks, fried them, placed them into a casserole dish, added a little plain tomato sauce, some black olives, and grated Parmigiano and pecorino cheeses, and tossed it all together to be baked for tomorrow's dinner.

At night I made risotto with butternut squash and sea bream. It was fine but I was distracted because my guests, dear friends that I had not seen in almost four years, and I got caught up in conversation. I was chatting too much to remember timings and neglected to even make a vegetable or a salad. They didn't seem to care but I did, and my lack of focus plagued me the rest of that sleepless night.

November 25

Thanksgiving. Or rather, today is the day we celebrate Thanksgiving since we left America, because obviously in England Thanksgiving is not a holiday. So, on the Saturday after Thanksgiving, fifteen to twenty people descend on our home (can people who are invited *descend*?), some of them family, some American expats, some American actors here for reasons I've stated before, and some just British friends who like to eat. Why do we do it? Because we like turkey? No. Frankly those busty, fatless fowls are a pain in the ass to cook, even though somehow Felicity has found a method of cooking them brilliantly. But we do it, we celebrate it, though it's based on the specious account that the Pilgrims and the Native Americans shared a meal together as a gesture of goodwill before the former decimated the latter's numbers through disease and genocide. And although that gesture amounted to nothing more than just one fleeting feast before it all went tits-up (or breast-up if you're the turkey), the idea of communing through food is beautiful and something to be celebrated.

People always think of the turkey when they think of Thanksgiving, but to me it's the side dishes, the trimmings, those ubiquitous "fixin's," that make that day's meal wonderful rather than the big bird itself. I see the turkey as an adjunct to the other dishes. That said, it's the *leftover* turkey, when artfully made into an open-faced sandwich with lots of gravy the *next day*, that floats my boat. Of course, I also partake of the remaining side dishes then as well. Here is what we usually make on the day of giving thanks:

A turkey (obvs)

Cranberry sauce (homemade)

Brussels sprouts with pancetta and/or chestnuts

Pigs in a blanket (store bought)

Devils on horseback (dates wrapped in bacon; store bought)

Green beans

Dauphinoise potatoes

Roasted carrots and maybe parsnips

Corn bread

Bread stuffing with water chestnuts and celery and other stuff I can't remember (my mother's recipe)

Baked sweet potatoes

Baked beans (sometimes; Kate's recipe)

Salad

Cheese board

Figs, nuts, and fruit

Apple pie or tarte Tatin

Wine (both colors)

As successful as it was, and as much as I love my friends and in-laws, I'm not so sure I would do it again. At least on that scale. It was two days of preparation. We rented tables and benches because our dining room table was not large enough to accommodate nineteen adults (whose is?), as well as linens, dishware, and glassware to make the cleanup easier, and besides, we didn't have enough tableware that matched. Let's face it: unless a mismatched table setting is consciously curated, it just looks like you don't have enough tableware that matches, which is exactly the reason it looks like that. I was so tired by the time I sat down to eat that I barely ate. The food all turned out well for the most part, except for the turkey, which resisted all of Felicity's culinary charms and was very uninteresting. Unfortunately, this turkey was like an uncomfortable first date. You know pretty quickly that it's never going to work out, but you're stuck at the table together till the end of the meal, so you might as well make the best of it.

November 26

With the help of our overnight guests, Danny and Monique, we broke down the tables and benches and continued cleaning up what we had not finished the night before (which is always so much more work than you think it's going to be). As a thank-you to them, I made omelets, which we ate with toast, avocado, cheese, and gorgeous, silky Italian mortadella that they had bought at a specialty shop. Some of the best I've ever had outside of Bologna. After they left, we continued cleaning, and finally we ourselves left the house at noon to shop for new tableware, because ours is old and its numbers are dwindling due to too much breakage over more than a dozen years. (Hence the aforementioned lack of matching pieces.) We went to Borough Kitchen, which is basically the Williams Sonoma of England, and found some very nice and surprisingly affordable stuff. Felicity and I should never be set loose in a place like that, but the children's moans kept us from overstaying and overspending.

We took the kids to see a film. It is very rare that we go to the movies these days and I'm sad about that fact. I used to love going to the movies. But the accessibility of films on streamers has made it a rare outing for so many, including those of us who loved going to the movies so much we devoted our lives to making them. I must make an effort to take the kids more often, as it can and should be a magical experience. After the film (which unfortunately was not a magical experience—oh, how I love those streamers), we popped into an antique shop, and I splurged on a vintage Arne Jacobsen stainless-steel tray, ice bucket, and tongs. My parents have the same one, although larger, and I've always loved it. Classic Scandi design is something that this aging Italian cannot ever get enough of. As it was so cold and damp when we returned home, I made a big pot of minestrone soup and *spaghetti con tonno* at Felicity's request. Matteo, Felicity, and I had the spaghetti. Matteo had three helpings. I wish my parents had been there to watch him devour it. It was like something out of a Pasolini film. Millie had leftover pastina with butter and cheese, and we all ate together as the soup bubbled away, to be eaten over the next few days. (Truth be told, three hours later Felicity and I both ate some of it.) The soup had more depth of flavor than usual but I'm not sure why. It could have been the chicken stock we had made, or the cup of strained marinara I added, or the extra piece of Parmigiano rind I dropped in for good measure, but whatever the cause, it worked.

Speaking of film and food (regarding my Pasolini reference above), food is seldom used in English-speaking films the way it is in most European films. What I mean is that because food is not as naturally woven into the fabric of daily life as it is in, let's say, France or Italy or India, it is practically nonexistent on-screen. In fact, food seems to be almost disappearing from many American films altogether. I mean, superheroes must eat at some point, but we never see them do it. Even the Russo brothers, who are food obsessed (another reason I love working with them), didn't incorporate food into the great Marvel films they codirected, as far as I can remember. I must take this up with them. Basically, in most contemporary British or American films, unless it is a "food movie," food is of no consequence. The perfect commentary on this is Eddie Izzard's stand-up routine known as the "Death Star Canteen." Eddie acts out Darth Vader going to get himself some lunch in the canteen, where the server doesn't know who he is. It's one of the most brilliant comic routines of all time.

November 27

I ate scrambled eggs on buttered toast with anchovies and parsley after a much-needed workout. Wow. Tomorrow, I will make it with chopped hard-boiled egg, which will be even better.

I cannot get two recipes out of my mind the last few days. The first is something I concocted the other day, which was a take on a *pissaladière*. I sautéed two onions and three leeks in butter and oil, spread them onto puff pastry, dotted the whole thing with black olives, and baked it for thirty minutes. I love savory tarts and pies. There are endless combinations of vegetables that can bedeck puff pastry, short-crust pastry, or pizza dough. Sautéed onions alone on any of those is a meal in itself. Ina Garten, probably the most successful cookbook author and television chef in America (Emily and I have both appeared on her show because she's one of our food idols), has a recipe for a short-crust pastry tart with leeks, goat cheese, and fresh tomatoes that Emily made a couple of years ago and I have since become obsessed with. With a green salad and a glass of wine, a good tart is a meal for all seasons. (There's a dirty joke in there someplace but I don't have the wherewithal to find it, luckily for you.)

The other recipe is from my childhood and one I often long for. Not only because it's delicious but because it brings back memories of slow summer lunches with my parents and grandparents. It's a simple dandelion salad with hard-boiled eggs and a light vinaigrette my parents make. These days, dandelion leaves can be bought in stores, but years ago the first waves of Italian immigrants in Westchester, New York, would collect them from lawns or along the parkways that led to Manhattan. I remember seeing them as we drove down the Sawmill Parkway on our Saturday errands. Every mile or so, there they were: short, stocky, stooped figures, slowly making their way along the grass that grew on either side of the road, plucking the deep-green dandelion leaves that other people considered a blight on their manicured lawns. But to those old Italians, that bitter weed was a delicious, healthy part of their next meal. Not to mention the fact that it was free.

Over time the numbers of those resourceful people became fewer and fewer until they faded away altogether. Either they had become too old for such an activity or they had simply passed away. Their children had no need or desire to follow in their parents' footsteps and cull the natural riches that continued to grow next to a parkway that itself continued to grow, but only more congested with cars each passing year.

November 28

Went to the Marina Abramovic retrospective at the Royal Academy. Our friend Heinrich is now on the board. It was the first time a female artist's work has occupied the entire space. Abramovic has always found new ways to express herself through her art in so many mediums. Like Louise Bourgeois, she has never shied away from being controversial and never apologized for it, or for being a woman in a male-dominated world. And like Louise Bourgeois, she has had a huge impact on the arts. The exhibition was impressive to say the least. Did I like all the work? No. But that would be impossible. One can't like everything any artist does because what they create is ever in flux. Art is a process, and as viewers we are privy to that process. Sometimes pieces "work" and other times they "don't work," for myriad reasons. Inconsistency is integral to growth and change. Good art is ever-changing and therefore at times inconsistent. Art is the opposite of a Twinkie.

Afterward we headed to see Emily, Cillian and Yvonne, my publicist Jenn (who also handles Emily), and Jenn Streicher at their hotel, as they are in town for what will be months of press for *Oppenheimer*. We had a great time but didn't really eat much, just appetizers, and we stayed too late.

November 29

Jenn Streicher and Yvonne came for dinner. I made *pasta alla Norma*. I want to eat eggplant all the time now. Is that the cold weather? But it's not a winter vegetable. I think I just love it. Eggplant, or *melanzane* in Italian, has many varieties and is grown and eaten all over the world. In southern Italy and Sicily, it is put to brilliant use in so many dishes—like caponata, eggplant parmigiana, eggplant rollatini—or sliced and used as the wrapping for a *timballo* filled with capellini and meat sauce, or as a pasta sauce with Tropea onion and tomato, or a sauce with pine nuts and olives served with casarecce pasta. In southern France, it's a key ingredient in the famous ratatouille; the Japanese bake eggplant with miso (love); in Greece, there's moussaka; in China, it's prepared with spicy garlic sauce; and, and, and . . . You can grill it, fry it (breaded or not), bake it, roast it, sauté it, or pickle it. I love that it is almost meaty and that it has at once a bitterness and a sweetness, absorbs flavors so perfectly, and almost melts in your mouth when cooked properly. I get cravings for it all the time. Like right now.

November 30

Had dinner with Woody and Laura at Farmacy, a vegan place in Notting Hill. Had the mushroom parfait, which was delicious, and the garden pizzetta, which was a bit spicy but tasty, so Laura and I traded—I ate her artichoke pizzetta and vice versa. A white Gavi and a French pinot noir rounded off the meal.

December 1

I made a leek and onion puff pastry tart. I used a different brand of premade puff pastry than I had used when I made the *pissaladière*. This one required a quick blind bake (which I did not do), whereas the other one did not, and therefore this one was soggy. The flavor was good, but the texture was not. I instinctively knew I should blind bake it—of course I hadn't read the instructions—but I didn't, and I ended up with a soggy bottom, which is never a good thing, for tarts or people.

December 2

Went to Riva with friends because we can't go too long without going there. I had *pizzoccheri*, which is one of my favorite dishes. It's a recipe from Lombardy, the region Mr. Riva is from, made with buckwheat pasta, potatoes, garlic, cabbage, butter, Parmigiano, and Valtellina cheese, and served only in the winter months. I have written about it in *Taste* and cooked it on *Searching for Italy*, so I won't go on. But it was delicious. I could have eaten three helpings.

December 6

The War Child Wassail. It was the tenth anniversary of this event to support the charity. It is organized by Carey Mulligan and her husband, Marcus Mumford. Gillian Anderson was there as an ambassador, and a beautiful choir and Marcus Mumford performed. Jodie Whittaker was there, and I boldly went to say hello. She introduced herself and said it was nice to meet me. She had clearly forgotten that we had met before. I was devastated because *I* had *not* forgotten. She's a great actress but obviously doesn't have a great memory. (I'm kidding. This is what I will tell myself to assuage the pain of being unmemorable to her.) I did a reading of "Yes, Virginia, There Is a Santa Claus." Jonathan Pryce did a reading of "No Man Is an Island," beautifully of course, and a few of the countless people who have been helped by War Child recounted their stories. It was moving to say the least. One point six million pounds were raised that night. The most ever for that event.

December 7

Have been working on the stories for the new iteration of *When Is Stan Getting the F— Out of Italy?* with BBC Studios; we are beginning in Sicily. Our goal is to find interesting stories that will show aspects of each region that are more interesting than the bog standard. We are getting there. There are a lot of cooks, however, and the kitchen isn't that big.

Felicity had organized for me to be part of a book signing at the stunning Waterstones bookshop in Piccadilly this evening. Like the rest of London, the shop was bedecked in Christmas decorations, which made it even more special than it already was. The place was packed with shoppers buying books for Christmas presents, which was a reassuring and literal sign that literature is indeed a gift. I was terribly flattered that so many people had waited for so long for me to sign copies of my family's cookbook and my memoir, *Taste*. I was equally flattered to be counted among the other authors there tonight, including Dolly Alderton, Paul Whitehouse, Cressida Cowell (the brilliant author of Matteo's favorite series of books, How to Train Your Dragon), Stephen Fry, and Elizabeth Day, as well as Julius Roberts, my favorite new chef, whose book I have been obsessing over. I was so pleased to meet and fawn all over him. I didn't get a chance to say hello to the others I knew there, as it was so hectic, but we had a bite with Elizabeth and her husband, Justin, afterward. I had escargots, which were tiny and delicious, but they were served on small, round flatbread, which made me sad. When it comes to escargots, I prefer the traditional preparation and presentation. Snails with garlic, butter, and parsley served in those classic dishes designed especially for them, accompanied by a fresh, warm baguette. That, a salad, and a bistro glass of French white or red could happily be my last supper. If a last supper can be happily had.

December 8

Felicity and I spent the better part of the late afternoon setting up what is to be the living quarters for Matteo's new reptile, a chameleon. (The green anole we bought him months ago is not quite interactive enough, or at all. Matteo named her Scuttles, a moniker to which she has never lived up. And yet despite her disappointingly tepid personality, for some reason she still lingers in his room skulking around a dank vivarium.) Anyway, regarding the chameleon (whose name is Arthur, after Matteo's best friend, the voracious eater I mentioned earlier, who recently told me he thinks my pasta is the best he's ever tasted. I always liked him), it seems that this poor creature was abandoned by the roadside and brought to the veterinary clinic where my sister-in-law Susie, the youngest of the Blunt sisters, practices. Knowing Matteo's obsession with all things reptilian, she thought his room in our home would be the perfect place for the bug-eyed orphan. Not knowing the amount of kit and live food and the size of the glass enclosure required to house the thing, not to mention the expense of it all (I've paid less for a kid's semester of college board), we readily accepted. Also, Matteo wept with joy when the proposal was made, so who was going to say no? Yet, as we struggled to carry the little green fella's sizable glass palace, technically known as a paludarium, up the stairs, I wondered if, had we declined Susie's offer, a few tears of disappointment from my youngest son might have been a valuable life lesson. *I* certainly learned a couple of lessons today. One: don't be afraid to say no. And two: don't carry a huge, cumbersome, extremely f—ing heavy glass case up the stairs if you are over the age of sixty, even with your much younger wife's help, no matter how much you love your child.

When all was in place (countless hours later), I nursed the lacerations on my forearms and the stabbing pains in my sciatic nerve with a lovely glass of white wine and some steamed langoustine. We ate nothing with them, no salt, no butter, no sauce, no *nothing*, because they needed nothing, and we were probably too tired to lift even a shaker of salt. After a bit of hesitation, Matteo ate some as well, but then he swiftly announced he prefers shrimp to langoustine. We'll see what he says when next he eats shrimp. I suggested that perhaps tomorrow we move on to a diet of lightly braised reptiles. He didn't laugh.

December 9

I made *pappa al pomodoro* (Tuscan tomato soup). I love this dish because I love soup, as I've made abundantly clear, but also because if there is a single dish that exemplifies La Cucina Povera (the poor kitchen), it's this one. Its ingredients:

Garlic

Onion

Tomato, canned or fresh

Basil

Olive oil

Salt

Vegetable stock

Stale bread, without crusts

When all those ingredients are combined and prepared properly, the result is a sweet, tomatoey porridge-like dish that is as comforting as it is delicious. I, however, did *not* prepare mine properly, because I did not cut all the crust off the bread. If one neglects to do this, the crust cooks in the tomato broth and it becomes rather slimy. Not appealing at all. Once again impatience is my culinary downfall. I also put in too much crustless bread, adding insult to injury. I have made it well in the past and am determined to do so again. It's going to be a long winter, so there will be time. Never give up. Especially when it comes to soup.

December 10

We went to Anita and Heinrich's for a Sunday lunch. It took us forty-five minutes to get there because of the traffic, even though they live three miles away. The traffic has been awful since the Hammersmith Bridge closed four years ago. It is a major and necessary artery to and from South West London, and its closure has caused terrible disruption, not only on the roads but also to local businesses. The bridge is a landmark structure and cannot be repaired in situ. Apparently, the structural problems can only be addressed by dismantling it, sending it to the mystical island where old bridges are made new again or some such fucking place, repairing it, returning it to its sacred site, and reconstructing it. However, in four years I have seen no attempt by the dozens of workmen who are there daily to begin this process. Personally, I think they should cut the iron beast off at either end, put it on a barge, ship it down the Thames, plop it in a park, and turn it into a walkable garden. Then they should get the British equivalent of the Army Corps of Engineers to slap up a functioning bridge lickety-split so that everyone can get to where they need to get to in good time. I mean, the Empire State Building took only one year and forty-five days to build. Just saying.

Anyway, just before we ran out of petrol and I had practically grown a full beard, we arrived at Anita and Heinrich's house. The kitchen smelled wonderful, and I saw that Anita had prepared tomato sauce and meatballs. As we ate appetizers, she held up a package of spaghetti and a package of mezzi rigatoni and asked me which one she should cook. Before she'd even finished the question, I pointed to the mezzi rigatoni. She told me that the old Italian shopkeeper who owns the deli where she buys her pasta gave her the same answer, but only after a lengthy symposium on sauce-and-pasta pairings. (It's not just me and the old shopkeeper who are so specific about pasta-and-sauce combos, it's a cultural obsession.) Anyway, her food was delicious, and I had two huge helpings. It reminded me of the Sunday lunches we would have when I was young. The table was always so beautifully set, and we would usually eat something similar to what Anita made today. I do like a classic British Sunday roast, but endless bowls of pasta with *ragù* followed by meatballs, spareribs, and beef on the bone, cooked slowly in the *ragù* for hours until they melt in your mouth, are very hard to beat on a chilly winter's afternoon.

That evening I made the kids soft-boiled eggs with toast and sausages, which they devoured. Felicity and I had steamed chard with fresh tomatoes and some toast.

December 11

Felicity was out at a "retirement dinner." I didn't know sex clubs hosted those. The kids ate chicken cutlets, and I had pasta with the leftover chard. We watched a couple of short Christmas films. I tried to find the ones I grew up with made by Rankin/Bass in the sixties, like *Rudolph* and the one about how Santa came to be, but to no avail. I couldn't even find the original Grinch narrated by Boris Karloff. I am sure they're all lurking out there somewhere in the ether, but I am simply not capable of finding the right button on the right remote to bring them back for a nostalgic holiday visit.

Aidan called and I was so happy to speak with him. I miss him and Lizzie terribly. He told me that one of our closest friends has been diagnosed with prostate cancer. Luckily, it has been caught early. He will have surgery and that will hopefully be the end of that. The insidiousness of the disease is overwhelming.

My old life—what was once my life—seems so far away now. Because it is. I seldom see my friends in America due to the distance between us, our erratic work schedules, and the fact that I have a young family. I could pay a visit when I have a few days of downtime but because I travel a lot for work, I don't want to travel for pleasure unless it's with Felicity or as a family. Silly, I guess, because at this rate those dear friends and I may only see each other maybe ten more times before we die. It sounds dramatic but if you do the math, it's not. Strange to know that that is an actuality. Our time together once seemed like it would never end. We spent so many years in each other's homes, in restaurants, on sets, at each other's premieres for films or plays we were in or directed, celebrating each other's birthdays and countless New Year's Eves, all the while supporting each other as success and failure came and went, relationships faltered, illness insinuated itself, and death visited too soon.

Time stands still only when you are in pain.

We are going skiing in Italy in February. There we will dine at the Italo-Austrian table on such dishes as polenta, mushrooms, gnocchi, venison, and whatever else the denizens of the Dolomites want to feed us. Although I will probably have to remortgage the house to pay for it, I cannot wait to go. I know Fee is hardly jumping up and down about a ski trip, except for the prospect of the food, but I am sure she'll lure me to a tropical clime soon where she will swim freely and I will cling to the beach. I don't swim. I have had a lifelong fear of water. Perhaps because, according to my mother, I almost drowned in the Hudson River around the age of two. Of course, I don't remember it, but maybe some region of my brain does, and that has for the most part kept me out of large bodies of water and the deep ends of swimming pools for over sixty years. I admire people who have no fear of the water, but I guess not enough for me to learn myself. It's just not a priority of mine. Maybe in my next life I'll come back with gills.

December 12

Went to the British comedian Michael McIntyre's house for dinner, which from South West London is like traveling to Prague. They served a delicious roast chicken and proper British roasted potatoes. Michael and Kitty are very generous and warm. He is also one of the funniest people on planet Earth. Ever.

December 13

Saw Woody in his play *Ulster American*. Funny and dark. Woody was nervous about going onstage again after almost twenty years, but he needn't have been, because he gave a truly great performance, as did the other two actors. Had wine at the reception and ate leftovers when we came home. I wish Woody and Laura would move here. I am on a subtle mission to get the American actors I've written about in the previous pages to relocate to London. Maybe not so subtle because I often will just blurt out, "Please move here!" Embarrassing sometimes, but truthful.

December 14

I had some sort of "bug" that was not allowing me to keep anything in my stomach. Didn't feel ill at all but Imodium was needed. Ate very bland food, which makes me a bit sad. I am sure, dear reader, that you're thrilled I've included that information in these pages. TMI? Perhaps. But I have been told that Proust also wrote similar passages, he just had good editors. I mean, I *cannot* believe that madeleines really sat *that* well with him.

December 15

Richard and Cheryl were supposed to come to dinner, but I had to cancel due to a bout of labyrinthitis, which is basically extreme vertigo that is incapacitating and can last for hours, days, or weeks. I always carry medicine with me that usually stops it pretty quickly. A shame, because I had bought a huge piece of bavette that I had salted and pounded out and was going to serve with an anchovy cream sauce from Julius Roberts's book. While I lay down for a bit, Felicity cooked some of it and made the sauce, and we ate it in front of the TV watching *The Christmas Chronicles 2* with the kids. I do love Kurt Russell and Goldie Hawn. You'd have to be an asshole not to.

December 17

My daughter Camilla returned home for the holidays. So good to see her looking so healthy. She has been skiing and has taken up rock climbing as well. The latter being not the easiest of sports to learn or for the climber's parent to learn how to deal with. But she's good at it and loves it. My fears should not be hers. She was understandably exhausted as it is a long flight from Idaho, where she goes to college, to Seattle and then to London. We had spareribs that Felicity had made that were a bit overcooked, which is not something she does often. (Children distracting a great cook once again.) I made Kate's recipe for baked beans, which were almost good. There was too much liquid in them. They need to be viscous, not runny. After Millie stopped talking Camilla's ear off and she and Matteo went to bed, Camilla, Felicity, and I ate together. The quality of our cooking was of no consequence because we were so happy to have Camilla back home and at the table once again.

December 18

More Zoom meetings with BBC and National Geographic for the show. Things are falling into place. We will be shooting in Sicily one month from now. Hard to imagine but I am anxious to get on with it. Too much talk can kill a thing before it's even brought to life. In the afternoon Felicity, Camilla, and I went Christmas shopping. Then we had an early dinner along with Nico at a new Chinese restaurant called Canton Blue, where we had a delicious cold sake, steamed dumplings, pork belly, and Peking duck two ways. Everyone in my family loves duck, and Peking duck is one of our favorites. Sadly, it is often overcooked and becomes just dry, gray shreds of flesh that you wrap in a thin pancake and slather with hoisin sauce to choke it down. But when cooked properly it just falls apart in your mouth and has the rich, greasy skin still clinging to it; it is a real delicacy. I had it in Beijing, and it was otherworldly. I love to see them hanging in the windows of Chinese restaurants, glistening with oil and fat, waiting to be hacked apart, shredded, and devoured. Poor things, it's like they die twice.

December 19

Took the kids Christmas shopping in Wimbledon. I've never spent much time in the village, and it is charming. Felicity is making a concerted effort to actually *go shopping* instead of ordering everything online, and I'm all for it. I like shopping. Always have. I have difficulty buying things online, not only because I'm technically challenged but because if I can't see or touch something, I can't really know if it's what I want because I don't really know what it is. Is the color of whatever I'm buying as dark or as light as it seems in the photo? Unless you've already *seen* the thing or already *own* the thing, you're never sure it's a thing you really want.

Anyway, we shopped and got lots of gifts for lots of people. We also went into an amazing butchery where we almost overbought but restrained ourselves. We left with four veal escalopes (with which I planned to make veal Milanese that night), four hamburgers for the kids, and three marrow bones. I did make the Milanese that night, and the veal was good but not as sweet as it should have been. It really should be quite pink when raw, and this was very red. Andy, who used to work for us, and Lottie came for dinner, and Camilla ate with us as well. Then Andy's son Aaron came by, as did Camilla's friend Ella. We had finished the veal, but as they were hungry, I made them some capellini with leftover marinara. They were as happy to eat it as I was to make it for them.

December 20

This week is going slowly. Did one of Monique's thirty-minute HIIT sessions. It was difficult, but it's like beating your head against a wall; it feels good when you stop. Afterward we went to our friend Amy's mother's funeral. Her mom, Valerie, had been struggling with early-onset dementia for close to five years. Heartbreaking. It's so hard to watch someone you love as they decline, but the decline from Alzheimer's can go on seemingly forever. And there is no drug and no amount of love that can stop it.

The house was empty when I came home as Felicity went on to the reception after the funeral. It was so quiet, something our house seldom is. I ate the leftover capellini with marinara and scrambled eggs. I thought about Valerie, who was only ten years older than me. She was half Italian and the few times that we met, we talked about Italy quite a bit. Her own mother was from Naples, met her British husband in Italy just after the war and moved to England with him. Valerie closely resembled some of my father's mother's relatives and I always wondered if we were somehow related. She was seventy-three. An age I once thought was ancient. Now I know it's far too young.

Had dinner at a nearby new restaurant with Jamie and Millie. Good appetizers but my entrée was not good. Four very large gnocchi on a bed of oversmoked, overcooked eggplant and tomato sauce. I do prefer the classic small gnocchi rather than the larger ones, because unless they are made by a master, they are always heavy and claggy (which is British for too dense and sticky). When made well, gnocchi are delicately light, and can be paired with countless sauces. They go equally well with a pesto as they will with a Bolognese, or with sage butter as they will with marinara. Felicity continues to make some of the best gnocchi I've ever had. I won't even attempt.

The children are beside themselves with excitement about Christmas. Since the beginning of December, they have been running directly to their advent calendars as soon as they awaken to find and devour whatever treat awaits them behind the door numbered with that day's date. We have also decorated our Christmas tree, which looks beautiful. I can't stop staring at it. As we were decorating the tree, I realized that Millie had crossed a significant threshold. I noticed that she no longer clustered all her chosen ornaments in one small section like all children up to a certain age do. This year she saw the tree as a *whole* and placed each ornament with purpose and precision on a number of different branches. It was fascinating to see her concentrating so hard, staying completely focused on her task and at times stepping back to take in the tree in its entirety and suggesting to me spots where ornaments should be placed. She saw the tree in the same way she has begun to see the world. She is beginning to understand that for equilibrium to exist in any form, one thing must complement another.

In the original German lyrics of "O Tannenbaum," the branches of the tree are described as "*treu*," which translates as "loyal" or "truthful." I always thought that was so beautiful. It was the tree itself that was the symbol of strength and faith. Not God, not Jesus, not the angels, not three wise men, not Mary, not Joseph, not the North Star. Just a tree.

I love not only Christmas Day itself but the buildup to it, especially when there are kids in the house who still believe in Santa. I don't want to think of our home in a few years' time when that belief has disappeared from their hearts. I remember when it happened to the older kids, and I was crushed. The winter after Kate had passed away, I took Nico, Isabel, and Camilla skiing in Deer Valley, the resort we would take them to every year. The four of us were on a chairlift and Nico finally plucked up the courage to ask me the fateful question.

"Dad, can we just ask you . . ."

"Yes?"

They all exchanged looks.

"Um, we were just wondering if, um . . . is Santa . . . does Santa really exist?"

A pause. My heart was breaking. Their mother was gone and now Santa would be too. I took a deep breath.

"Well, I don't know if Santa exists or not, but I will always believe in him."

They exchanged looks again and then smiled.

"Okay."

And then we arrived at the top of yet another mountain.

December 22

Emily and John and the girls have arrived. They will be here for Christmas, which makes *everyone* very happy, especially the children, who are literally bouncing off the walls. They rented a house around the corner from us, and after they dropped off their bags, they came to ours at about nine p.m. and we fed them pasta. We all stayed up too late, including the kids.

December 24

We hosted a lunch for the Blunt family and a few friends. I made gravlax a couple of days before, which turned out well, but it could have cured for another day. We served oysters from France (don't know what type but they were delish), and Felicity made Julius Roberts's chicken pie, and everyone was very well sated. I did however miss the fish fest that my family always served on Christmas Eve. I was hoping to make a fish stew, like a cacciucco or cioppino, or even a bouillabaisse, but Felicity nixed that idea because she said most people don't like fish stew. I thought about pushing back, because a part of me doesn't really care if people like fish stew or not and I like the idea of sticking with the Catholic tradition of not serving meat on Christmas Eve (even though I am very un-practicing), but everyone at the table was Church of England (although also very un-practicing), so I didn't really have a leg to stand on. However, there is something so pure about a meal of primarily fish, especially the night before one will be confronted with potentially two meat dishes and all the sides that go with them. Anyway, the gravlax and the oysters were the only sea creatures that we ate, and though I hate to say it, Felicity's chicken pie was great.

In the evening Nico and Camilla helped Matteo and Millie lay out food for Santa and his reindeer. This is the menu they chose:

Carrots

Cookies

Chocolate

A clementine

A shot of scotch (at my insistence)

Millie also wrote a note for Santa telling him that she loved him.

After the brushing of teeth, the reading of stories, countless questions, and theories about how Santa *actually* fits down the chimney, I sang off-key renditions of a few Christmas songs and Millie and Matteo were finally tucked into bed. Once they were soundly asleep, we carried their well-hidden gifts downstairs and placed them under the tree. Nico and Camilla, proudly continuing a tradition they grew up with, placed a new stuffed animal at the end of Millie's and Matteo's beds and made a trail of chocolate coins that the next morning will lead them to the Christmas tree, now practically obscured by a plethora of presents.

December 25

Christmas morning, we opened the plethora. Nico and Camilla were excited to watch Matteo and Millie tear open their gifts as they themselves once did over a decade ago. Nico made waffles for them with the new waffle maker I bought and then made the rest of us scrambled eggs. (They were so creamy I thought they must have had butter and cream in them, but he used only oil and salt.) He also made bacon, toast, and one large crispy hash brown, which we shared. So nice to have a chef in the family.

It was also nice to have the two generations of kids together, but we were all sorry that Isabel was not there. Although knowing she was with my parents was reassuring.

In the afternoon the Blunt-Tucci-Krasinski clan ate at Susie and her husband Charlie's house, where we indulged in ham, roast beef, stuffing, turnips, green beans, and you name it.

December 26

I am still getting used to the idea of Boxing Day. It seems a bit unnecessary after the previous two days, but this is England, and as they say, "When in Londinium . . ." This year we did not spend it with family, although John and Em and the kids did stop by in the evening. Instead, Laura, Woody, and two of their girls came over and I made *spaghetti pomodoro*, Felicity made a green salad, and Laura made delicious sautéed mushrooms and a kale salad. It was Woody's day off from the play before he was to perform seven shows in a row, so he was in need of good food and good wine. Even if one isn't about to embark on a theatrical marathon, I believe good food and good wine are always a good idea.

December 27

We took all the little kids with Emily and John to see the musical version of Emily and Felicity's favorite childhood film, which shall remain nameless. It was almost fun. My belief is that not every book or play should be a film and not every film or play should be a musical. Obviously, there are exceptions, but most things should just be what they are. This was a prime example. Afterward we took the kids to the Ivy (I had the cottage pie) for an early dinner and then we went home for an early repose.

December 28

John and I headed out at eleven a.m. to spend the day and night at Guy Ritchie's country house. John is about to do a film with him, and Guy wanted him to visit so they could finally meet in person and told John to extend the invitation to me as well. I have always wanted to meet him as I am an admirer of his films as well as his sartorial style. After a couple of hours in the car—luckily John is great company—we arrived at one of the most beautiful properties I've ever visited. A series of old redbrick and stone houses sat in a bucolic setting of woodlands and green fields that spanned over a thousand acres. Inside and out, the buildings were immaculate in both condition and taste. They were not overly grand, but they had stature and bore the weight of their long history well. The weather was of course miserable, bitter cold coupled with lashing rain. As we got out of our car, we were met by a well-dressed young fellow who showed us to our rooms in two of the many outbuildings designed for guests. We dropped off our bags and hopped into one of the countless Land Rovers that were parked in one of the many driveways. From there we were taken to another part of the property, where a pheasant shoot was in progress. We arrived at a little dale, where there were eight people dressed in bespoke tweed suits, ties, and classic hunter green outerwear. It could easily have been a photo shoot for *Field & Stream* circa 1926. Guy greeted us with a wave and a smile from a distance. About ten minutes later, that leg of the shoot ended and Guy came over, shook hands with us, and welcomed us heartily. After being introduced to his wife, son, and group of friends, we all climbed into an antique wooden caravan with an arched roof. Inside was a long narrow table with a contiguous U-shaped bench. In the front of the carriage was a small refrigerator, hidden slyly behind a wooden door, and a small wood-fired stove for warmth or even for cooking if one so chose. John and I took our seats at the table and looked at each other in disbelief. Canapés were offered. I selected a small venison tart that was delicious and John a tiny pork pie, as we had barely eaten that morning. We willingly accepted the whiskey and beer on offer. We were beyond cold, as we were not really dressed appropriately for a winter shoot. I at least had boots and a rainproof jacket, whereas poor John was wearing a small down jacket and a thin pair of dress pants; he said, "It's like I'm wearing pants made out of paper."

As we sipped the booze, a few of the guests—some British, some American, but all longtime friends of the Ritchies—told me how much they loved *Searching for Italy*, especially a fellow named Jamie Lee. Jamie organizes all the high-end shoots for the upper echelon of British society. It is no wonder that he and Guy are best mates. They are both smart, darkly funny, and know and love food and drink on a par with many chefs I've met. They are also skilled cooks. After we chatted a bit and the whiskey warmed our cockles, the final phase of the shoot began. By this time the weather had taken a turn for the worse, which hardly seemed possible, and the warming effect of the booze was swiftly washed away.

Soon thereafter we were transported to the main house. Here we sat in a covered stone entryway next to a beautiful wooden case that held three small kegs of Guy's own brand of beer and ale, called Gritchie, which is brewed on the property. The ale was particularly interesting because it had no effervescence, which I was told was the way ale was made many years ago. It was a "live" brew and not allowed to ferment. It was smooth, slightly creamy but not thick, and gave one no bloat whatsoever. It was one of the best things to come out of a keg that ever wet my whistle.

After chatting for a bit, we headed inside to the living/dining area, where a fire was burning and a long table was beautifully set for twenty or so guests. That night we ate a smorgasbord of incredible food. Pâtés, salads, game, and a turbot the size of a small bateau cooked in a wood-fired oven. When the turbot was brought to the table, I pointed out the beautiful char on one section of it. Guy, who strives for perfection in so many aspects of life, including at the table and the bar, asked me if the turbot shouldn't have a bit more of that char on the rest of it. I said without a doubt, as long as it didn't end up being overcooked. He looked at me for a moment, eyes widening, his gaze practically boring into my skull. Then all at once he slapped my shoulder and said, "Let's go." He leapt up from the table, grabbed the plank that held the turbot, and stormed toward the kitchen with me following suit. John looked at me as I passed, eyes filled with questions, and I smiled as I whispered, "The fish." He nodded politely, as though to say, *Of course*. I entered the kitchen, which was not that large but was incredibly well designed and outfitted with everything a cook or chef would/could/should ever need or want, including a substantial wood-burning domed oven in one corner. I practically soiled myself. There were about four chefs/cooks working away like mad making more and more gorgeous dishes. We swept into the kitchen, Guy clutching the wooden plank that held the turbot like a battering ram, and the sea of chefs quickly parted. He grabbed a long-handled steel pallet, scooped up the fish, and slid it expertly into the oven. There was silence as we both stared at it intently, and then after less than a minute, he took it out again and we assessed the char and feel of the flesh. "What do you think?" he asked, eyes even more intense. "Turn it around and give it another twenty seconds," I said. Having full faith in my culinary expertise (little did he know), he followed my suggestion. After twenty seconds he removed it. The char was more even over the whole fish and the flesh still supple. We popped it back on the plank, brought it over to the kitchen island, and, forgetting about the other guests, tore off piece after piece of the slightly oily, crackled, charred skin and moist, silky meat with our hands and shoved it into our mouths. No plates, no utensils. Just hands.

Like the fellow in the video eating the snakes.

Eating with your hands.

Why have we been dissuaded from doing so?

It's great.

Eating a huge fish with your hands that has just come out of the fire.

Extraordinary.

Eating a huge fish with your hands that has just come out of the fire on a cold night in a historic house in the English countryside.

With Mr. G. Ritchie.

Fuckin' extraordinary.

I rue the day the Italians invented the fork.

The meal ended with whiskey and other digestives being poured as the Ritchies' friend Sam, an expert in ancient folk songs, sang a few of them beautifully to a well-sated and rapt audience.

The next morning, we breakfasted at the same table we had dined at the night before, and the first meal of the new day rivaled the last of the previous evening. Homemade focaccia (the best I've had since filming a segment about the stuff in Genoa a year and a half ago), fruit, coffee, juice, and a full English breakfast consisting of creamy scrambled eggs, tomatoes, mushrooms, plump sausages, beans, and ox tongue decadently fried in butter (and that's no yoke) were all on offer. Smoked salmon was brought to the table as well, but Mr. Ritchie dismissed it as it looked a bit anemic, and he wasn't unright.

After that lordly meal, we hopped into a couple of cars with Guy, Jamie, and Sam for a tour around the property, which consists of 1,100 acres of undulating fields and woodland. First, we made our way to the brewery. I imagined a small affair with a few old-fashioned fermentation vats and barrels, but what we were introduced to was very much the opposite. Housed within an enormous, meticulously renovated multiroom stone barn sat a state-of-the-art brewery with stainless-steel tanks, pipes, valves, and vessels for which Anheuser would have mud-wrestled Busch. We never entered that brew room itself but instead just viewed it, agog, through the huge interior glass wall it stood behind. The rest of the place sported a professional catering kitchen, a pizza oven large enough to supply all of Naples with their favorite foodstuff until Vesuvius puts an end to it all, and two large halls for parties of at least a few hundred, all connected to room that held a twenty-five-foot-long bar and a seating area peppered with different styles of antique tables and chairs. Outside the bar there was a brick courtyard and a continuation of the stone barn that was once stables that Guy intends to turn into an outdoor cooking and dining area. John and I looked at each other shaking our heads, grinning, filled with admiration for our host and trying our best to suppress our covetousness. We returned to the bar and Guy pulled some pints of his own brew. These were very welcome to my brother-in-law and me as they took the edge off the emotional overstimulation. We sipped the ale and chatted about kids and family, and then Sam sang a couple more old ditties as the sun tried to break through the clouds and find its way into the hop-scented rooms of stone.

As we continued our tour of the property, we discovered that not only is Mr. Ritchie a talented filmmaker but he also designs furniture (based on military campaign designs), transportable wooden cabins (they stand on simple cast-concrete footings, have roofs that slide open so one can sleep under the stars, and can be constructed or broken down in a matter of days), tents (these are also based on officers' campaign tents and can stand alone or be connected to the cabins), and perhaps most important, cooking appliances the likes of which I had never seen. Well, that is not entirely true. I *had* seen similar ones before—in the Beckham documentary. The cooking tent and the iron, steel, and copper-clad barbecue equipment that old Becks was practically making love to, and I'm obsessed with, was designed by Mr. Ritchie himself. *Good Christ*, I thought, *what the f— is happening?!*

Sam soon left us to get a massage in the property's sweat lodge along with a few of the other guests, a practice that seems to be de rigueur on the Ritchie compound. We, however, headed to another spot by a lake, where there were a couple of different cabins and a "cooking tent" that contained one of the *double* barbecue apparatuses. We entered, and John and I stood awestruck by the copper cooking oracle before us. As Guy and Jamie adjusted the tent flaps to keep out the ever-strengthening wind, I noticed there was a thick piece of something wrapped in white butcher's paper. Guy then grabbed a bag of charcoal (he makes his own; who doesn't?) and loaded it into the barbecue. The barbecue was rectangular, about eighteen inches long, twelve inches wide, and eight inches deep; sat within the copper tabletop; and was vented by a slim stainless-steel chimney at one end. Within fifteen minutes the coals were white-hot, and Mr. Ritchie unwrapped the white paper, revealing a thick, marbled rib eye, and slapped it onto the grill. We drank a French red and discussed the finer points of this brilliant apparatus and the accompanying tools dangling from the stainless grid connected to the chimney and suspended above us. From it also hung individual round wooden cutting boards with rounded handles at either end. Each rounded end was concave and connected by a groove that ringed the entire board. One of the hollowed-out round ends was for salt and the other allowed for the juices to pool. Containers of napkins secured in a holder also hung upside down so that they might be easily accessed, because at this table one would often eat with one's hands. Mr. Ritchie told us that as we cooked the steak, which he had been turning constantly with a pair of tongs, we would "chip away" at it. What he meant is instead of cooking it and then placing it on a board, cutting it, and serving in the usual manner, we would begin to cut it piece by piece from the outside edges inward, then return it to the fire to continue cooking. This would ensure that the steak was cooked consistently all the way through, as opposed to the outer part being more cooked and the inner parts less cooked. Using this method, the meat eaten would always be hot and cooked to perfection. Mr. Ritchie handed me the tongs and asked me to do him the honor of finishing off the steak, and I did. He then took it off the grill, slapped it on one of the cutting boards, filled the groove and one hollow of one handle with the juices and the other hollow with salt, cut slices from the sides of the steak, laid them on the board, passed it around, and told us to eat it with our hands. And we did. It was one of the best steaks in both quality and culinary execution that I have ever had. The remaining steak was then returned to the grill to continue cooking.

As the temperature dropped, we took little notice due to the wine and the steak, but also because the barbecue is specially designed not only to cook but to heat your legs, which tuck comfortably under the tabletop. John kindly abstained from drinking more than a few sips of wine, as he was to drive us to meet our wives and children at a house he and Emily had rented in Sussex for the week between Christmas and New Year's. Could we have stayed all afternoon chipping away at the steak and sipping away at the wine? Yes, and yes again. But reality beckoned, and it was time for us to take our leave.

When John came to my room to help me load my bags into the car, I looked at him and asked the unanswerable question: "What is happening? I mean, what has just happened?"

He smiled as he effortlessly hoisted my heavy suitcase with his six-foot-four frame as though it were cotton candy (strapping, handsome, talented bastard with nice hair) and shook his head. "I don't know. I . . . I just don't know. But I mean, that was . . ."

"I know," I said. "I know."

We said our goodbyes to our more-than-generous host, the talented Mr. Ritchie, and drove off to meet our families in another part of the English countryside. There would be no pheasant shoot; no tastefully decorated bedchambers; no full-time chefs; no bespoke tweed suits; no campaign furniture, cabins, or tents; and certainly no custom-made copper-clad cookers with which to barbecue the perfect steak and warm your legs at the same time. We would be wrangling children, begging them to tell us what they wanted to eat, making something that approximated their requests, and cleaning up after them. I will not pretend for a moment that we didn't consider concocting a tallish tale about engine trouble forcing us to stay another night. But neither of us is that kind of fella, and the desire to see our families was too strong and our love and devotion too powerful to make us stay, even though the siren scent of grilled meat and gunpowder lingered, trying its best to convince us otherwise.

The last few days before New Year's Eve were spent with Em and John and their kids, Danny and Monique, Stephen Merchant and his lovely partner, Mircea, and my daughter Camilla. The weather continued to worsen, so except for a long walk one day, we were hunkered down inside, exercising, cooking, eating, etc., etc. As usual we seldom saw the children except at mealtimes. We did however teach them how to play Articulate for Kids, which was more than funny.

December 31

I drove Camilla to the train station, as she was headed back to London to spend New Year's Eve with her best friend Ella. I was sad to see her go but knew we would be together again in a couple of days. That night after a dinner of Emily's stupidly delicious homemade cottage pie, we put the children to bed and sat by the fire, and chatted about whatever we chatted about. The stroke of midnight was imminent, and I could feel the vibrating strings of anticipation among us. Even though I am no longer interested in big bashes to ring in the New Year (well, maybe every now and again because I love to wear a tux), there is always a little flutter in my heart just before the stroke of twelve and a surge of hope that the New Year will bring betterment. I could sense that none of us knew what to do when that moment came other than raise a glass and toast to 2024, and I thought something more was needed. I suddenly found myself telling everyone to don their coats and hats, as it was a very cold and windy night, and to meet me out on the patio. I grabbed a bottle of champagne and some candles, hurried outside, placed them in a circle on the old gray stones, and somehow lit them in the relentless wind. A few moments later everyone emerged and instinctively encircled the candles. I had created the circle of candles to echo the campfire we used to build on New Year's Eve in upstate New York outside Aidan and Lizzie Quinn's home. It was there for almost two decades that Kate and I; Steve Buscemi and his late wife, Jo; and an ever-revolving group of friends would welcome the New Year. We stood around the fire every

December 31, never imagining that there would be fewer of us so soon and that this tradition would not continue forever. Now, here, in a different country with new family and other friends, I felt the need to re-create the essence of that ceremony, if even with just a few candles in the howling wind. When everyone had gathered round and just before the clock struck twelve, I popped open and poured the champagne, raised my glass, and blurted out a toast. I toasted to all of us there in that moment, to those we loved but who were not with us now, and to those who were no longer with us but whom we would never stop loving. I toasted to our children and *their* children and expressed hope that they will carry on sharing and celebrating love for and with their families and friends when we are no longer here.

And then we counted down. And then it was midnight. And then we hugged and kissed and wished each other a happy New Year. And then someone put on the recording of "Auld Lang Syne" from the end of *It's a Wonderful Life*, and we sang along as we sipped the champagne in the miserable English weather and silently wondered what the next year would bring to a wonderful but ever fractious world.

January 2, 2024

The New Year is here. John, Em, and the girls are leaving for the States. When the cousins said their goodbyes there were more than a few tears, especially from the younger two. I saw Millie's chin quivering as she hugged Violet and when they separated, they both let forth unabashedly. We all reassured them both that they would see each other in a few months, which, to children of that age, sounds like a lifetime and feels even longer. But soon the tears abated and the Blunt-Krasinski family was heading out of the drive on their way to Heathrow. We left not long afterward and drove back to London with heavy hearts but a lighter load because we'd eaten and drunk the majority of what we'd packed. We would indeed be seeing the Blunt-Krasinskis again, but not until the end of the dreary damp known as an English winter. Within the next few days, Camilla would be on her way back to college, Nico would be manning his station in the restaurant, Isabel would be returning from her stay with my parents, Matteo and Millie would return to school, and Felicity and I would start work once more. Suddenly it seemed that the year had passed very quickly, even though during the midst of it there were times when it seemed it might never end. But it's always that way. It's like heading to a place you've never been to before. Because you don't know where you're going, the trip seems so long. But when you return to that place again, the same trip will seem so much shorter because now you know where you're going. Or at least you think you do.

Epilogue

January 2024

During the first week of the New Year, as we reentered the pattern of daily life, Felicity and I made a concerted effort to break our practice of feeding Matteo and Millie first, putting them to bed, and then making a separate dinner for ourselves. We decided to push dinnertime a bit later and all dine together, knowing that because they had after-school activities almost every day (gymnastics, soccer practice, ballet, and so on), this would require a few snacks to sustain them until dinner. So, some combination of breadsticks, oranges, sliced salami, bananas, prosciutto, pistachios, and Goldfish (brought over by Em and John on one of their visits) was meted out judiciously to sate them temporarily. I am happy to report that it was and continues to be a great success. So much so that last week Matteo said, "I like it so much better when we all eat together." So do I.

Postscript

The other night I finally had a dream about food. In the dream I was looking at a magazine filled with recipes and one of my daughters was next to me (which daughter was unclear). The recipe, albeit strange, was straightforward; therefore, even though it was in French, I could understand it. The magazine had a photo of the dish during one stage of the process surrounded by all the ingredients. I translated it for my daughter and commented to some woman who was there (I've no idea who she was) that it looked interesting and seemed simple compared to many French recipes, and the unknown woman agreed with me.

The recipe called for a large eel to be stuffed with ground beef, carrots, onions, celery, garlic, salt, and herbs, then rolled, tied, and baked.

When I awoke the sun was rising. I lay in bed thinking of the bizarre concoction my sleeping mind had let loose. A recipe for stuffed eel fit for a medieval monarch. What did it mean? A huge eel. Why? Then I wondered what Freud (who consistently ate steak tartare throughout his entire life) would have said about my dream. Possibly something like:

"Herr Tucci . . ."

"Yes, Doktor?"

"Was there any sex in this dream?"

"No."

"Any death?"

"No, no."

"Hmm."

Freud thinks.

"You know, Herr Tucci . . . maybe sometimes an eel is just an eel."

I nod.

Freud picks up a pack of matches. "Do you mind if I smoke?"

"The eel?"

We both laugh.

DAS ENDE

Acknowledgments

My editor, the wonderful Helen Garnons-Williams at Penguin/Random House, and her team:

Ella Harold
Richard Bravery
Rose Poole
Jane Gentle
Emma Brown
Annie Underwood
Meredith Benson
Samantha Fanaken

My equally wonderful editor at Simon & Schuster, Alison Callahan, and her team:

Sally Marvin
Aimée Bell
Jennifer Robinson
Taylor Rondestvedt
Mackenzie Hickey
Lisa Litwack

And of course, Jen Bergstom.

I thank them all for their support, great humor, and patience.

The hardworking literary gang at Curtis Brown:

Flo Sandelson

Emma Walker

Rosie Pierce

Sophie Baker

Katie Harrison

Tanja Goossens

Lottie Birmingham, for being a great business partner and friend.

My extraordinary publicist, Jennifer Plante.

My diligent agents Franklin, Oriana, Carly, and Santini, and my manager, Tony.

Amanda Bross, who brilliantly handles all things branding.

Dear friends and family whom I've mentioned within these pages.

My parents, Joan and Stan, for their inspiration in all good things.

My children, for their kind hearts and curious appetites.

And especially Felicity, the smartest person I know and whose idea it was for this book, for her selflessness, kindness, positivity, encouragement, and love.

Now I see that it must be almost as difficult to live with one's client as it is to live with one's agent.

Almost.

About the Author

Stanley Tucci is an actor, writer, director, and producer. He has directed five films and appeared in more than seventy others, countless television shows, and a dozen plays on and off Broadway. He has been nominated for an Academy Award, a Tony, and a spoken-word Grammy; is a winner of two Golden Globes and six Emmys; and has received numerous other critical and professional awards and accolades. A lover of all things culinary, Stanley cowrote and codirected *Big Night*, the critically acclaimed movie about two brothers running a failing restaurant; starred in *Julie & Julia*; and was the host of the three-time Emmy-winning series *Searching for Italy*. He is the author of *Taste: My Life Through Food* and two cookbooks, *The Tucci Table* and *The Tucci Cookbook*.